D1109417

TRANSFORMED BY THE LOVE OF GOD

JOHN WALKER

A MAN FOR THE 21ST CENTURY

——— TRANSFORMED BY THE LOVE OF GOD ———

JOHN WALKER

A MAN FOR THE 21ST CENTURY

Robert Harrison

FORWARD MOVEMENT
Cincinnati, Ohio

© 2004

Forward Movement
412 Sycamore Street, Cincinnati, Ohio 45202
www.forwardmovement.org

Forward Movement, an official, non-profit agency of The Episcopal Church,
is sustained through sales and tax-free contributions from our readers.

Contents

Sermons, Addresses, Letters/Prayers

Sermons

Addresses

Letters/Prayers

Foreword

He was a man, take him for all in all,
I shall not look upon his like again.

—Hamlet *I. ii.*

I greet you as John Thomas Walker's son. More immediate and intimate to my father, certainly, but since he considered the whole church—actually all of God's children of any faith, or even no faith—his extended family, I welcome you as brothers and sisters. My father never met a stranger.

In the pages of this book you will get a glimpse of the warmth, compassion, faith, and care the public Bishop John Walker exhibited to the world. I am so pleased that this effort will enable many who never knew him to learn something about his extraordinary life and witness to some of the extraordinary events that shaped the world. Literally. I am pleased, too, that it will serve as a reminder to those of you who did know my father to see yet again some of his spiritual journey.

No person can be adequately described or captured in words on paper, so I wanted you to know some of the private, human side of my dad to portray what he was like. Though very much a public person, one who engaged presidents and world leaders, the U.S. Congress and, of course, people throughout the Anglican Communion around the globe, my father was always available to his family. Clergy families generally share in the sacrifice of the often absent clergyman attending to priestly duties.

Without exception, however, none of us ever felt cheated of his time, presence, or love. We do not have any idea how he managed to do that—but we know we received from him constant attention and affection.

We also know everyone he came in contact with felt the same way. He had that rare ability to make whoever he was with feel as if they were the most important person in the world to him. People that knew him were nurtured by his sensitivity and his loving and caring nature. People came and stayed with us so often it was not unusual to think that our family was much larger than it was. Our friends came to the dinner table frequently. They, too, found in him a willing listener and counselor. He affected the lives of countless young people who came probably expecting an icon instead of the very genuine and caring man they encountered.

My mother will say it was ever thus, from the moment they first met in her hometown, Limon, Costa Rica. Word had traveled to her town that some students and teachers from the United States were in their country for a summer program of teaching and working with the Church. She also heard of one particularly striking and handsome young priest. She was, she says, smitten the moment she saw him. After a local dance they met and talked. And talked. And talked some more—and he walked her home.

He came to visit her again and then he returned to the United States. They corresponded and the following year he returned to see "his Maria." Not long after he came with a ring, and a proposal. She calls their relationship a "love affair enduring," and when she said she was afraid to go to the U.S. based on all the stories about racism she had heard, he said to her, "I'll protect you."

He took his new bride to his cure at Saint Paul's School

in New Hampshire and she says it was a glorious time. Her fears about the United States ended in the comfort of John and in the community of the school.

There were aspects of my father's life about which people would have no clue. Most who knew him, or knew about him from afar, would never have guessed that this powerful man—Washington powerbroker and insider, confidant of Presidents and the famous—had anything other than a privileged life. Yet he was flesh and blood and, a black man in a time when racial equality was nowhere near a reality. He was the youngest of three sons that survived to adulthood from the nine children of Mattie Wych Walker. Despite her heartaches, she gave to him a sense of the wonder and mystery of God. She played the piano and sang hymns to him from his earliest days in Georgia. A sharecropper's son, he was brought up in what we would call poverty of a kind that ought not to exist anywhere. But my father never spoke of those times as if he and his family were poor. For his parents instilled in him a deep respect for the value of others—*regardless* of their color, or lack of color, or how they treat you—and a life-long pursuit of knowledge and the value of that knowledge.

My father never met a person he could not find some good in. He never carried a grudge—even against foes who openly tried to undermine him or his authority. His willingness to continue to work with people who had opposed or even betrayed him, underscored his strength of spirit and character.

Many of his acts of love and kindness go unmentioned anywhere. He would never grandstand and tell others what he was doing. That was not his style. He assumed guardianship of his brother Joe's three children. He cared for Joseph, Burke, Patrick—his nephews—as if they were his own children. He was very close to his brother Henry, his wife Maxine, and their daughter Kathy. He and my mother gave a home to many, and our family served as both a magnet and shelter to all sorts and conditions of people. Maria will say John was as unfailingly available to a person down-and-out as he was to a president.

To us, his children, my father would talk movingly of his own childhood and youth without ever mentioning the hardships he and his family experienced. My mother says of him that there simply was no bitterness or complaint about the injustices he faced many times in his life. He taught us as he lived: always see the best in others.

As a child, growing up during the racially volatile '60s my father offered this advice: if you ever come home and find no one there, and the doors locked, just sit on the front steps and wait until someone returns to open the house. Never try to enter through a window or push through the back door—it just might make a passing policeman or neighbor nervous, and they might harm you. My father repeated this advice to me over the years, but it was only when I was a teen that it occurred to me what he was telling me. Because you are black, you are subject to a different kind of justice and profiling.

We lived an extraordinary and happy life. My father taught us, too, that one must define oneself, not allow others to define you for you. When we visited Africa for the very first time it was an overwhelming experience. It was the first time in our lives that, as people of color, *we* were in the majority. It was a powerful realization for us. My father's concern for the poor and the injustices faced by Africans—whether by whites in apartheid South Africa, or by despots strangling the life and liberty of their own people—was a reminder, too, of human nature and that oppression is a world wide epidemic. It served to give him great resolve in fighting the injustices done to people, wherever they might live. In this arena, John Walker caused the world to quake and think anew of the possibilities of the brotherhood of all humanity.

John Walker had an impact on the world's conscience. He not only ministered to his own flock—whether as priest and Master at St. Paul's School, a parish priest, Cathedral Canon or as Bishop—but to the world as a whole. World events and history would place him in a role to affect some of the key events in our nation's struggle for equality for all people, and in the Church's growth and inclusiveness. That his life and witness brought him into direct contact with Martin Luther King, Jr., Archbishop Desmond Tutu, and correspondence with Nelson Mandela on the one hand, and American political leaders—both pro and anti-civil rights—on the other, enabled his unimpeachable integrity to effect change in laws, policies, and lives.

My father would not live to see the real end of apartheid, but he knew it, too, would fall—just as all unjust laws and even nations that support tyranny will eventually crumble. He would be so proud to know how much the world has changed. He would be patient, masking well his *impatience*, to see further restrictions on the liberty of people melt away.

My father had no fear of death, because of his faith in God and his deep belief in the ultimate goodness of God, and of the Resurrection. So many have mourned his too-early death. But we also have nothing but joy and thanksgiving that this remarkable man lived at all, loved us so well, and never gave up on any true and Godly pursuit. We loved his stories, his great laughter, his great sense of humor, and his good natured teasing. He was a source of joy and wonder for each of us. Busy as he was, he was never too busy to be with us.

We never believed we had to share him with the world; we are just grateful that God shared him with us. Now, we are grateful that you, too, can get a sense of this man we called husband and dad.

—Tommy Walker

Rosa Maria Flores Walker
Thomas P. Walker
Ana Maria Walker Caskin, M.D.
Charles Nathan Walker, M.D.

John Walker—
Bishop in the Church of God

Every Sunday since the 1988 Lambeth Conference I have prayed for a special group of people by looking at the picture taken of us on the grounds of the University of Kent where the conference was held. The picture is of the bishops who were members of our Bible and discussion group. Bishop John was one of this group. Three of those in this photograph are no longer alive. Amongst other things, the picture reminds me of the quiet but significant influence that John Walker had on that Conference. The Archbishop of Canterbury, the late Robert Runcie, had a special committee that met each evening after the day's proceedings to assess how things were going and to make suggestions about possible changes in the next day's agenda to facilitate the work of the Conference.

John Walker was one of the few non-archiepiscopal members of this crucial committee which had those quaintly named persons, the Primates of the Anglican Communion, each of whom headed an autonomous ecclesiastical province of our communion. I was always fascinated to note how frequently after Bishop John had spoken on any particular issue, that often signaled the end of the discussion. He had a quiet, gentle but undoubted authority to which most of our Church seemed quite willing to defer.

I seem to have known him forever, for he had that gift of making you feel special, that when he was engaging you there was nothing more important for him in the whole wide world. He gave you all of himself, and you were for him then the most important person on whom he would lavish his total undivided attention—allowing nothing to distract him from this important task. He was a devoted and caring pastor because he genuinely loved people and poured himself out for them constantly. So, I do not recall when I first met him, but from that moment on we clicked. He cared enormously for people, especially those who were having a raw deal: the poor, the hungry, the despised, and down and outs everywhere.

Bishop Walker cared that so many of God's children were having a rough time, being destitute and poor, everywhere…in the USA, in Africa and elsewhere. So he volunteered to go and work in Uganda. Then he was involved in the antiapartheid struggle and gave us his formidable support from the strategically important Diocese of Washington and the National Cathedral. When I became Archbishop of Cape Town, he helped to forge a three-way relationship between our dioceses as well as the diocese of Honduras, and cared that it was not all rhetoric—our third world dioceses benefited enormously from being so prominently linked.

It was a great joy to have him and Mrs. Walker visit Cape Town for my enthronement as Archbishop. They were deeply moved by what they saw of the ravages and iniquities of the repressive system of apartheid, and this reinforced his resolve to work assiduously for the demise of that awful system. He wanted the world to know this and so gave me a prominent pulpit from which to speak about our agony and our hope for the future. Perhaps it was this kind of prominence that helped to protect me from the machinations of the apartheid regime. He cared for all of Africa and poured out relief through his beloved Africare.

I was privileged to attend his funeral in the Cathedral he loved so dearly and whose completion was such a fitting tribute and memorial to him. I was so touched by the many people of all races who were weeping unashamedly in that huge congregation who had come to pay their last respects. It was clear that they adored him, and the service was people of all races, for one of Bishop John's passions was racial justice, harmony, and reconciliation.

Although he was fervent in his opposition to racism, Bishop John had the knack of opposing evil without alienating the people caught up in it. He was not abrasive, although he was not wishy-washy, either. He was a splendid advocate for racial harmony and reconciliation, and the willingness to be magnanimous and forgiving and understanding—the very attributes we were to see demonstrated so spectacularly by Nelson Mandela and the many victims of apartheid in the Truth and Reconciliation process that has been working hard to heal the deep wounds of my own country's history.

God gave us a marvelous person in his servant John Walker. When he died, he undoubtedly heard his Master say 'Well done, good and faithful servant,' as he stood before the Gates of Heaven. We are all the better for having been touched by him; the Church of God is a more effective fellowship as a result of his outstanding ministry and witness.

We welcome this biographical anthology of his work.

The Most Rev. Desmond Tutu
Archbishop of Cape Town,
South Africa (Emeritus)

Up and Down the Hill

Who shall ascend into the hill of the LORD?
or who shall stand in his holy place?—Psalm 24:3

Ordinarily you won't see a Bishop running anywhere, much less down a steep hill toward a football game, dressed in his purple shirt, pectoral cross wildly swinging. But this was no ordinary bishop. From his office on Mt. St. Alban, the Rt. Rev. John Thomas Walker, Sixth Bishop of Washington, was on his way to watch his older son play one afternoon on the school fields at the foot of the National Cathedral. He was late, as usual. So he ran. As he went careening down the hill, he fell. It was most undignified. Most men would have cursed, but this Bishop most likely came up laughing. He recovered gracefully, executing a neat forward roll. He sprang back, and without missing any other stride, tore off again downhill toward the gridiron.

No one would have ever known about his trouble, but one of his son's teachers had been watching the bishop's progress, unobserved, from his office at St. Albans School. Yet no one who knew John Walker would have been that surprised by the story, either. John Walker was a family man, a man committed to the lives of children; a graceful man, a private man, a very busy and important man, a good-humored man, a man moving fast because he had lots of ground to cover.

From the beginning he was different. From the start, he had a lot to prove. His father thought of him as his family's runt—not much good for hard work or baseball. But a light shone in his eyes; he thought in poetry. What he lacked in size and strength, he made up for in speed. He knew instinctively that if people were not expecting much from you because of how you looked, you could prove them wrong by working harder.

John Walker's journey to the top would take him from a small town in Georgia, through inner-city Detroit, to an exclusive New England prep school. He would walk hand-in-hand with children from poor villages in Costa Rica and Uganda, and he would sit down in serious conversation with the late twentieth century's most powerful men. He would guide the Episcopal Church through a decade that saw historic reform in its worship; he would ordain one of its first women priests. He would preside over the dedication of the sixth-largest Cathedral in the world, whose multi-million dollar construction deficit his fundraising campaign had decisively erased. He would be considered for his Church's highest office. He would be a pastor and spiritual friend to thousands, each of whom felt wholly understood and uniquely cared for when he stopped to talk.

Walker's accomplishments and spirituality are celebrated by those who knew him. And yet John Walker walked through the world with a profound sense of wonder and humility. He found himself, often reluctantly and usually without design, inserted into some of American history's most important scenes. If you had been there to see it at the time, you might not have known it was happening, until a distinctive limousine would pull up exhibiting small American and Presidential flags on its front bumper. It was not unusual at the Walker household for the Secretary of State to phone, as Cyrus Vance once did, to ask for the Bishop's advice, say, about lighting the national Christmas tree during a time of international crisis.

Born the great-grandson of slaves, driven by his father's pride from the unrepentantly unreconstructed South of the 1920s, drawn with his family to the industrial heart of the Midwest in the Great Migration; a child of the Great Depression, a laborer supplying the Arsenal of Democracy in World War II; a witness of the Detroit race riots of 1943; disillusioned college student, recipient of the "white man's largesse"; angry worker for civil rights in Mississippi, friend of Martin Luther King, Jr.; John Walker stood with police to calm violent young men in the streets of Washington in 1968; he sat in council with President Jimmy Carter to decide the future of the Panama Canal; he watched as Egyptian President Anwar al-Sadat received back from Israel the Sinai Desert mountain where, tradition has it, Moses received the Word of God.

In decades to come he would lift his voice as an advocate for the powerless in an era of imperial excess and runaway military spending; he would witness and, with his friend Archbishop Desmond Tutu, help to bring about the demise of apartheid in South Africa; he would smash the barriers that separated one-half of the human race from full participation in the ordained ministry of the Church, co-consecrating Barbara Harris as the first woman bishop in the Apostolic Succession—the unbroken line of faith and authority that extends two millennia to encompass the most intimate followers of Jesus.

This dynamic journey of faithful reflection ended abruptly in 1989 when Bishop Walker died suddenly in office. Five thousand people mourned him in the Cathedral he saw finished, celebrating his legacy: concern for social justice, for the life of America's great cities, and for the future of Africa. He had taught and organized the education of the world's elite and the nation's most easily forgotten children. He had brought races, faiths, and nations together in common cause.

John Walker was a reconciler, a bridge-builder whose influence extended well beyond the confines of the Episcopal Church. As a leader in ecumenical and inter-faith relations, Walker's vision reached out to embrace a fellowship of all believers. As a founder of the Interfaith Conference of Metropolitan Washington, Walker united faith communities in the nation's capital to learn from each other, to promote economic justice, and to defend human dignity.

It would be overstatement to claim that John Walker personally facilitated the racial integration of the Episcopal Church, or opened all orders of its ordained ministry to women. Nonetheless, he was quietly instrumental in doing both, and the Church he left behind in 1989 was a world away from the one he entered in 1947. Walker was in the forefront of efforts to include women, ethnic minorities, and people of all sexual orientations fully within the life and ministry of the Church. In doing so, he drew deeply on his own experience as a civil rights pioneer. He personally desegregated a seminary, a prep school, and a fashionable private downtown business club. His Cleveland Park home was the first (and for many years, the only) African-American household that his black friends could visit in the white neighborhoods that popu-lated the western side of Rock Creek in Washington, D.C.

He broke new ground wherever he went. In 1953 he "scandalously" attended the wedding of seminary class-mate A. Heath Light, who would later become Bishop of Southwestern Virginia. The wedding party had to be carefully briefed lest they cause a scene when a black man came down the receiving line. After the marriage ceremony, the assembled reception crowd held its breath in a private club until the town's *grande dame* held out her hand, and welcomed him saying, "You must be John Walker. We are glad to have you here." His presence won her over, and she would not be the last.

John Walker took to heart his parents' foundational belief that education was the door to opportunity. The door nearly closed for little, young Johnny Walker who had the audacity to learn to read before he arrived in Miss Lewis's kindergarten class. When school began, he read a page aloud instead of coloring it as he had been told. This infuriated her. She focused on him mercilessly to the point the black child was locked in the closet one day. He was released only after his mother went to the school to find out why he had not come home with the other children of their neighbors. Remembering the story without acrimony, Walker used it to help explain why he worked unceasingly to see that the next generation of gifted African-American students would find the doors of every educational institution in America open to them.

From his roots in Depression-era Georgia to his championing of social responsibility before the U.S. Congress, John Walker moved steadily toward ever more aggressive advocacy for the poor. He confronted head-on the "Reagan revolution," giving voice to those left behind in an increasingly economically divided America. The idea that in this country—or any other, for that matter—a child could be hungry was, in Bishop Walker's words, "simply unacceptable." The point, he said, was not only to bless the poor, but to feed them.

As dedicated as he was to what, in an earlier age, would have been called domestic missions, Walker was committed to service abroad as well. The people of Africa weighed heavily on his heart from the time he set foot in Uganda as a young priest assigned to teach in that needy diocese's theological school. Much later, he would train new African bishops who faced the daunting task of caring for a continent being torn asunder by its encounter with the modern world. Walker served from the early 1970s until his death as Chairman of the Board of Africare, a leader among private, charitable U.S. organizations assisting Africa.

Walker always understood intuitively the relationship between relief and politics. His ministry brought him into frequent contact with what St. Paul called the "powers of this age." He was intimately involved with complex negotiations and legislation involving Central American and African affairs. In the years when Oliver North and Nelson Mandela lived in the headlines, John Walker made it the Church's business to understand and to speak about Central American freedom fighters and South African opponents of apartheid.

There are those who found the bishop's meddling in secular affairs unseemly. Many, especially older and more socially conservative Episcopalians, thought religion should not interfere with politics. Of course, John Walker knew that the action (or inaction) that flows from religious convictions was inherently political. He was an observant student of history who knew that politics—especially American politics—could be unabashedly religious. His own cathedral existed as testimony to this intermingling. Its congressional charter called for it to be "a great church for national purposes." John Walker carefully defined the parameters of a concept that was inherently contradictory in a republic and a religious community mutually committed to the separation of church and state.

Over the years Washington Cathedral had been the site of many national observances. Anti-war protests, prayer for national calamities, celebration of success has all been staged within view of the Bishop's chair inside. President Woodrow Wilson is entombed in a crypt in the south bay of the aisle of the nave. So in some sense, Ronald Reagan was not out of line when he selected the National Cathedral as the preferred venue for his second inaugural prayer service. He ran straight into John Walker, though, when he chose a prominent fundamentalist as his preacher of choice.

Ultra-conservative Christians, after all, had been instrumental in winning the president a second term. On the tightrope he walked between church and state, Walker held the Canterbury Pulpit to be above the politics of electoral religion. Walker approved Reagan's second choice, perennial favorite Billy Graham, put forward as a compromise candidate, but insisted that Graham's homily be submitted in advance for his approval, which it was—much to the Rev. Mr. Graham's chagrin.

This incident throws in sharp relief the relationship between politics and religion that Walker held in such creative tension. He masterfully balanced the distinct halves of the Cathedral's mission. Guided by his own convictions, Walker saw that televangelism and partisan agendas were not going to be confused with the proclamation of the Gospel.

That is not to say that John Walker shied away from controversy. On a springtime Sunday in 1968, just days before his assassination in Memphis, and long before he was acclaimed a national hero, the Rev. Martin Luther King, Jr. preached in the Cathedral at the invitation of John Walker. Dr. King delivered his sermon from the same pulpit where Jerry Falwell would not be welcome.

Pastor, teacher, cathedral builder, civil rights leader, ecumenist, social justice pioneer, urban missionary, relief worker, statesman, politician—the titles are impressive in their scope. His resume can still impress as well: Rector of St. Mary's Church, Detroit; Master at St. Paul's School; special missioner for the Diocese of New Hampshire; Canon of the Washington Cathedral (1966–1971), then (from 1978 until his death) its Dean; first chairman and guiding light of the Urban Bishops Coalition; first president and driving force behind the formation of the Interfaith Conference of Washington; chairman of the Black Student Fund and longtime chairman of the board of Africare; member of the boards of Virginia Seminary, St. Paul's School, and the Church Divinity School of the Pacific; Suffragan Bishop of Washington (1971–1977); Sixth Bishop of the Diocese (1977–1989); candidate in 1985 for Presiding Bishop of the Episcopal Church, an election he lost by just ten votes; honorary doctorate degrees: L.H.D., D.D., S.T.D., LL.D., some of them twice over.

It is all too easy to list the titles and miss the man, for he was not much interested in titles. For all the access his office and his accomplishments brought him, Bishop Walker remains most remarkable for his ability to bridge the gap between the public life of official Washington and the intimate spiritual lives of its most powerful inhabitants. A powerful man in a city that revolves around power, Walker wore his authority lightly. He lived modestly, spoke quietly, listened carefully. Those who knew him never questioned his faith or his convictions. People from drug addicts to denominational executives relied on him to negotiate the path successfully on which it was possible to think critically, to act wisely, and passionately to believe—all at the same time.

He was handsome and beloved, a true romantic and

bachelor into his mid-thirties when a beautiful and determined girl in Costa Rica set out to grab his attention. Within six months they were married. When his bride-to-be arrived for the first time in the United States just days before the wedding in Detroit, he was stuck in his New Hampshire school dealing with one student crisis or another. He was chronically overextended, bearing the burdens of others, trying to do too much. His health suffered for it. Yet even those closest to him were usually unaware of the burdens he bore so gracefully.

Walker was one of those rare, genuinely real people who was unaffected by money, power, and prestige. Here was a man who ironed his own shirts. He carried his youngest son on business trips with him. He circled the globe and roamed around his diocese from one corner to another, received an armload of honors, and balanced the competing needs of a score of organizations. He prayed and preached in all the most important places. Yet all he ever really wanted to do was come back home to help with his children's homework and maybe, on a rare Sunday off, to sneak away and take communion quietly in a chapel of his cathedral.

What most people remember about John Walker is this gentle family man, a man who laughed and loved to tease. Even as his power and authority increased, he was without pretension. He had a way of making anyone feel welcome. Over the years, he and Maria and their three obliging children took in many strays—not dogs and cats, mind you, but stray people. Crime victims found a refuge in the Walker's home until they felt safe enough to start rebuilding the security of their own. Friends of friends passing through stayed over for a few days. Family from Detroit or Limon, Costa Rica were frequently in residence. Folks who were between houses or waiting for a job to come through, came to dinner and left a few months later.

Diplomats who had been called back home dropped their children off to live with the Walkers while they finished their school term; one young man stayed into a second decade. Prostitutes and alcoholics would seek out the preacher they had seen on television, and he would sit for hours on the porch, listening to their troubled stories. (Some were in such a state that he was afraid to let them in the house!)

Those who sought out John Walker longed simply to be near him, to be heard, cared for, and forgiven. They wouldn't go away until he came. One destitute man came banging at the door one night only to find that Bishop and Mrs. Walker were in South Africa. A panicked call from their teenage son arrived in Cape Town asking what to do. Neighbors were summoned to assist, but it took the Cathedral's security force to convince the importunate man that Bishop Walker couldn't help him then and there.

In light of all he did, to praise his accomplishments and his personal spirituality risks sounding fulsome. In the days following his death, he was called "magnanimous in spirit," "a powerful and effective force for change," "a remarkable man," "one of the great bishops of the Church." Such words would surely have embarrassed him, as would the prospect of his own words growing with relevance and importance. He was a soft-spoken man. He was, as one admirer noted, quiet.

But not silent.

In a tribute released not long after Walker's death, Pamela Chinnis, the Episcopal Church's ranking layperson, wrote this:

John Walker's legacy to us—whether we be women, blacks, young persons, or builders of cathedrals—is the conviction that what may seem impossible can be possible if we, like him, are faithful witnesses of the God of justice and compassion to an often indifferent world, and an occasionally indifferent Church.

She had it right. John Walker's life is a compelling story of how one good man can change the course of history.

Would that there were ten more like him today.

Chapter 1

Fellowship of Believers

I pray...that they all may be one.—John 17:21

For John Walker, the human experience was pro-
foundly spiritual in its own right, a self-authenticating
acknowledgment of God's existence and ongoing power
in the world. And, while he was a faithful son of the
Episcopal Church and a scrupulously orthodox Christian
priest, John Walker was also a champion of our common
humanity and a firm believer that his own tradition had
no corner on the marketplace of truth. On these two
powerful convictions he created structures of ecumenical
and interfaith cooperation that continue to grow and
prosper, and he affirmed a central place for the ministry
of the laity that is practically without equal in the modern
Church.

When Bishop Walker died in 1989, the Walker family,
the diocese, and the Cathedral received countless expres-
sions of sympathy. Letters, cards, and telegrams poured
in from around the globe. The high and mighty and the
nearly anonymous sent tribute. Few were as telling as the
letter that Walker's successor opened from the Spiritual
Assembly of the Baha'is of Washington. Their secretary
hailed the late Bishop as a "true spiritual leader whose
very presence encouraged the development of those
nascent aspirations toward spirituality that we all
possess." She noted that his influence "extended far

beyond the confines of his chosen Church, to persons everywhere who yearn for courage and nobility of spirit in their leaders." John Walker would have read the words with a modest smile, considering it a note from a good friend.

From his early life in the multi-ethnic neighborhoods of Detroit, Walker encountered human beings in their wonderful and confounding social and religious diversity. Early in his ministry as Cathedral Canon he built on his personal experiences in South America, Africa, and New Hampshire—which was, in its own way, no less exotic a place for an aspiring African-American clergyman in the early 1960s. By 1971, the year he was elected Bishop Suffragan, he was a leader in efforts like Inter-Met, a community-based practical education program for seminarians of multiple denominations. It functioned as a community training center for newly-ordained clergy. One of Inter-Met's goals was for its students to share their divergent religious philosophies. Walker, for instance, saw that it was a place where white seminarians could encounter the riches of "black theology" in a sympathetic environment.

By the second year of his episcopate, Walker was moving in high-profile interfaith circles as well. In September 1972, just days after the massacre of Israeli athletes at the hands of Palestinian terrorists at the Olympic Village in Munich, Walker was called to speak. He gave a message at the Memorial Service held by the Reflecting Pool in front of the Lincoln Memorial, ground hallowed by marches still fresh on the minds of the nation. His words drew the praise of the Jewish Community Council (and its 165 affiliated organizations) for their ability to "communicate to the world...[the] collective mourning of the religious community."

By the time Walker assumed responsibilities as diocesan bishop in 1977, his administrative assistant needed several pages to spell out his involvement in ecumenical and community affairs. Even after editing, it is an impressive list: board member of the Council of Churches of Greater Washington, Chair of the Washington Ecumenical Training Center, monthly participant in the Ecumenical Cabinet (a meeting of Protestant judicatory heads), Vice Chairman of Africare, former Chair of the Black Student Fund, D.C. Commission on Judicial Disabilities and Tenure, Police Chief's Advisory Council, Advisory Committee of the Regional Addiction Program, member of the national Episcopal Church's Joint Commission on Ecumenical Relations, Delegate to the Fifth Assembly of the World Council of Churches (Nairobi, Kenya 1975), Chairman of the Study Commission on Military Chaplaincy and the Committee on National and International Problems; Board Member of the Absalom Jones Theological Institute (Chairman), Interdenominational Theological Center, Virginia Theological Seminary, Association of Episcopal Colleges, St. George's College, and D.C. Bicentennial Commission; speaker at the University of Pennsylvania, U.S. Naval Academy, North American Congress on Alcohol and Drug Abuse, Foreign Service Institute's Workshop for Families, and the U.S. Army War College.

In the first two years of his tenure as diocesan, Walker made ecumenical affairs a prime concern of his ministry. He skillfully wielded the tools at his disposal both to craft cooperative alliances of groups and individuals and to create enduring institutions and organizations. It is a model of leadership Walker used time and again not only to advance his own agendas, worthy as they were, but also to draw in other visions that would deepen and extend what he always thought of as his own imperfect understanding. He used the power of personality, the extensive network of relationships he had built over a decade of dedicated service to the Washington community, the resources and prestige of the National Cathedral, and his visibility as a successful African-American leader in the predominantly white world of the Episcopal Church to effect substantial and lasting change.

Nowhere is Walker's heartfelt genius at building communities of faith and action more apparent than in his seminal work in founding the Interfaith Conference (IFC) of Greater Washington. Drawing together twenty-nine executives from twenty-four different institutions representing Christians, Jews, and Muslims, Walker convened a meeting at the Cathedral College of Preachers on December 13, 1977. His "top-down" leadership paid off as the leaders of these faith communities organized themselves for an unprecedented venture in ecumenical and interfaith cooperation. Within nine months, the group was incorporated, and by January 1978 it had launched a program to address the problems of the aged, criminal justice, human rights, economic justice, world peace, and cooperation. Both in its message and its mode of operation, the IFC has been, and continues to be, a strong reflection of the man elected to be its first president, John Walker.

The Interfaith Conference is the first staffed organization in the world to unite Islamic, Jewish, Christian, Baha'i, Hindu, Jain, Latter Day Saints (Mormons), and Sikh faith traditions. It is widely recognized as the standard against which other interfaith organizations are measured. In its first year, the IFC tackled the issue of infant mortality in the nation's capital. Their work was instrumental in bringing the Special Supplemental Nutritional

Program for Women, Infants, and Children (WIC) to the District of Columbia, the last jurisdiction in the United States to accept malnourished, poverty-stricken expecting mothers into a program that the federal government had made available nationwide six years earlier in 1974. From its inception, the IFC spiraled out to create or to participate in the creation of active community organizations including the Capital Area Community Food Bank, the Coalition for the Homeless and Housing Organizations, the Religious Freedom Roundtable, and the Campaign for a New Community. Its programs include environmental pilgrimages to the recovering Anacostia neighborhood in southeast Washington, workshops and trips for high school students, congregational partnerships, a speaker's bureau, the Commission on Social and Economic Justice, lectures, concerts, dialogues, and prayer services. It is the ministry of John Walker multiplied a thousand times over.

During Walker's tenure, the IFC addressed attempts by the federal government to eliminate tax exemption for churches involved in social action, ongoing crises of the District of Columbia's government that threatened major curtailments of social services, the Reagan budget cuts of 1984, nuclear arms control, and the AIDS crisis. What links these disparate topics is the universality of their claim for the attention of people of faith and their place in the heart of John Thomas Walker.

When John Walker preached about a major topic of concern on Sunday, the newspaper reported on a statement from the IFC on the same topic Monday morning. The skeptical might see this as an example of a large ego manipulating levers of institutional control, and craftily employing the power of the press to advance its own. But it would be more accurate to explain the confluence as a genuine man's ability to discern paths of cooperative activity and, knowing that with enough people, they could embark together so that they just might be able to accomplish something for good, maybe even something for God.

In his interfaith and ecumenical ministry, the secret of John Walker's success was his uncanny ability to balance cooperative action and prophetic confrontation. He seems always to have known when and with whom to disagree, when to work toward reconciling opposing points of view, and when simply to close his eyes to disagreement in order to get on with the job. His sensitivity and skill in making that discernment made him a valued member of any organization, an effective bishop, and a world leader in the ecumenical movement.

In 1978 and 1979 the Bishop of Washington used his position to make bold statements about the importance of religious cooperation. Before the winds of Vatican II died down, he asked the Roman Catholic College of Cardinals to admit ecumenical observers to the conclave in which they went on to elect Pope John Paul II. (They said, "No." Perhaps they already felt obliging enough since the previous Pope had recently spoken to the Archbishop of Canterbury for the first time in four hundred years.) He spoke to the National Press Club about the need for people of faith to work together for the good of their community. He went to the White House with the delegates of the Third Assembly of the World Conference on Religion and Peace to hear President Carter confirm his own belief that the religious community was humanity's most powerful force for peace in the world.

In an era that has come to be remembered most for the re-emergence of religious fundamentalism, John

Walker stands out for his universalistic morality. Walker appears in retrospect as one of those extraordinarily rare people who could lead a particular community of faith while understanding that community to be only one path toward believing. To describe him in terms of moral psychology, he was a post-conventional thinker whose practices and beliefs flowed from a principled conscience rather than from adherence to a set of rules. Walker was always able to see above the fray, to identify common ground, and to move others gently in that direction. Indeed, his convictions would lead him to break any number of both written and unspoken rules in his day. But always he moved according to his conviction that followers of all great religions were the channels through which flow the healing of the world.

So much of what is touted as interfaith ministry amounts to little more than "Let's just be nice to each other." No doubt it is a sentiment with which John Walker would have agreed. But being nice, he knew, was not enough. In 1979, the Third Assembly of the World Conference on Religion and Peace issued a Declaration that reads like a manifesto for Walker's life and work. Their basic convictions read like John Walker's own:

> We pledge ourselves to continue to grow in our mutual understanding and our work for peace, justice, and human dignity.
>
> We know that the forces which negate human dignity are all around us. We see the menace of deadly nuclear weapons and desperate national insecurity. Technological and economic power often exploits and excludes the poor of the world. Political power often represses dissidents and denies human rights.
>
> World community, built in love, freedom, justice, and truth, is another name for peace. It is

the goal of all our striving. It is not a utopian dream… In our various religions, we know that we are members of one human family. Sustained and motivated by the spiritual power by which we all live, we believe that there is an alternative to violence. We believe that peace is possible.

The power of active love, uniting men and women in the search for righteousness, will liberate the world from all injustice, hatred, and wrong.

Their vision of a responsible world community pointed them toward precisely those areas which John Walker dedicated his life: economic justice, nuclear and conventional disarmament, human rights, and education for peace.

∞

As Bishop, Walker never shied away from using his authority to act, and he exercised a ministry of visionary clerical leadership that remains a model in the Episcopal Church and beyond. But always he knew, and he always worked, in a way consistent with the knowledge that his role was not the only one, nor even the most important one. That distinction he bestowed on the lay people of his diocese. Part of Walker's genius was his understanding that to achieve his universal vision of reconciliation, he needed all the people of God.

Partly because his vision was so expansive, Walker highlighted and encouraged the ministry of the laity throughout his ministry. In 1980 Walker launched a major initiative designed to enhance and promote the role of lay people in the Church's mission. In the late twentieth century, the Church came to a renewed understanding that the real work of ministry is accomplished not by priests and preachers in church on Sunday morning, but by ordinary Christians in the workaday world. Many clergy gave lip service to what was (in some circles) a radical idea; most continued to act as if "ministry" was the exclusive domain of the ordained. John Walker served the laity by creating the Cathedral College of the Laity.

A half-century earlier, the foundation overseeing the operation of the National Cathedral and its associated institutions had established a College of Preachers. Its intent was to serve the laity by improving the quality of what they heard from the pulpit week by week. But the first College's mission remained focused on ordained clergy. The second College looked toward the other 99% of God's people: the laity. Its mission was to ask and answer practical questions about the workday integration of religion and public life.

In 1985 the College of the Laity became a full member of the Episcopal Cathedral Foundation, joining the College of Preachers and the three Cathedral Schools as a tangible symbol of John Walker's commitment to lay ministry. The College was an interfaith endeavor. Among its accomplishments was a groundbreaking study with corporate executives. The study set out to explore moral character and how it functions in, and is developed by, the workplace. Imagine: seventeen senior managers—bankers, insurers, lawyers, accountants, real estate developers—meeting five hours every month for a year, not to cut a deal, but to discuss how matters of the Spirit impact the day-to-day operations of corporate capitalism. That is what John Walker saw as the Church at work in the world.

The College did not long survive Walker's death and subsequent changes in the Cathedral's leadership. Yet its work lives on in sister organizations like the Washington Metropolitan Dialogue, prodded into existence by the spirit of Bishop Walker in 1995. The Dialogue is an example of Walker's continuing legacy in the city he lived in and loved.

Like all prophets, Bishop Walker stood at the dangerous edge between what is and what should be. Much of his ministry involved articulating for the Church a vision of what was both necessary and possible. He did not hesitate to call the powerful to task when their plans (however well-intentioned) moved outside the biblical mandate for justice and peace. But he was equally critical of the Church for its own failure to equip those in power for the vital ministry they perform in the world. When charity became confused with justice, Walker did not blame senators and presidents whose policies left the poor behind. He blamed the bishops, priests, and deacons who had not taught them better. He called for clergy to do their chief duty of equipping lay people for their ministry, providing those in high places (and those who chose them for those offices) with the Christian principles and reflective practices they needed to make just decisions and to formulate policies that lead to peace.

Walker fully actualized and called the Church to practice the biblical vision of ministry set forth by St. Paul in his letter to the Ephesians:

> But to each one of us grace was given according to the measure of Christ's gift... And He gave some as apostles, and some as prophets, and some as evangelists, and some as pastors and teachers, for the equipping of the saints for the work of service, to the building up of the body of Christ; until we all attain to the unity of the faith, and of the knowledge of the Son of God, to a mature man, to the

measure of the stature which belongs to the fullness of Christ (Eph 4:7, 11-13).

In this key passage lies the very heart of John Walker's ecumenical vision of cooperative lay ministry: each one given grace, the work of service, the building up of the body, the unity of faith, the knowledge of the Son of God, the fullness of Christ. It bears reflection.

This central vision of ministry some have seen reflected on the very walls of the Cathedral where John Walker presided over its setting into stone. In a sermon—by a layperson—announcing the formation of the College of the Laity, one preacher divined a mystery:

> At the end of the cathedral we have this beautiful carving over the altar, of the Christ in Glory holding the earth over which he reigns in his left hand.
>
> In a mysterious sense this Christ in Glory beckons to the extraordinary Frederick Hart sculptures at the other end of the cathedral, to be his partners in that dominion and reign. At the entrance to the Cathedral you have probably observed the unfinished Adam, or as we may more aptly describe, the Adam on his way to fulfillment; and above him in the tympanum, the eight human beings emerging out of the firmament…called into the public square to be his partners, called to be his Royal Priesthood in bringing his kingdom on earth as it is in heaven. That is his covenant and contract with the people of God. That is his commission to us.

It is a commission heard and lived out in the ministries empowered by the life of John Thomas Walker.

Several months before he assumed formal responsibility for the diocese from his predecessor, Bishop Creighton, John Walker had already begun to outline the direction of his episcopate. In this 1977 address to the annual diocesan convention, Bishop Walker defines the Church's mission in ecumenical terms and identifies the central role of the Episcopal Church on which he would build the effective interfaith coalitions that were hallmarks of his ministry.

Rt. Rev. Sir, Delegates to the 82nd Convention of the Diocese of Washington, guests, and friends: It is with some excitement and considerable apprehension that I offer this address as the Suffragan-Coadjutor Bishop of Washington. When next I offer such an address it will be as Bishop of Washington. Those words have an awesome and proud ring to them. But along with the pride and awesomeness there is the stark reality of the extraordinary responsibility those words carry. I have already learned as your Suffragan how great are the expectations laid before every Bishop and how frustrating it sometimes is not to be able to meet those expectations and fulfill them all. On the other hand, the simple awareness of limitations and the necessity to turn to others and to seek the guidance of the Holy Spirit is itself a comforting thing.

One of the expectations of a bishop is that he says something. Frequently the demand is very clear: "Don't tell us how bad things are, inspire us." Or, some say "the world is a mess, my life is a mess, and I don't know what to believe—if anything. I am a cynic. Inspire me—I dare you." Faced with such a demand one is tempted to say "forget it" or something stronger. But like all shepherds we struggle to find the word—not that by doing so we will cover the truth, but that we might reveal it with greater clarity. For we believe that hidden in the truth about Christ, there is the word to inspire, to uplift, to comfort.

My purpose today is to look at the point where the Church and the world touch, to see if we can discover what the mission of the Church is—what it can or should be during these next ten years.

It is not often that we have time to step back from what we are doing to look at our mission to see whether our activities do in fact touch the mission. We are in this diocese very richly blessed. We have experienced a period during which a great deal of time and energy has been given to our diocesan life. As a result we appear to be (and all the data support this conclusion) a strong, healthy diocese. It is on this premise that I propose that we look beyond ourselves at the larger mission.

Here again, we have been a diocese on the forefront of critical social and political change. We have also been involved in those changes that have happened within the Church. Our recent annual clergy conference revealed the extent to which we have been increasingly pulled and pushed into the arena of the world. Do not misunderstand me; we have often walked into the arena motivated by our particular understanding of the mandates of the gospel. Both nationally and locally, the Church found a coincidence between the world's agenda and its own.

Sometimes the intersection of our work and witness showed our mission and the world's agenda to be exactly the same; sometimes they were related only in a complementary way. The Church and the world have been concerned together about civil rights; racism; Vietnam; amnesty; changes in the moral climate (e.g., abortion, birth control, the sexual revolution, drugs); crime; education; the breakdown of the family; and perhaps most of all, a longing for peace.

Inside the Church, our agenda has been concerned with General Convention Special Programs; reparations; the Missionary Development Fund; internal racism—all of which are related to the world's agenda as well. But then there has been the revision of the Book of Common Prayer; the question of voting rights at General Convention; ordination of women; and the place of homosexuals in the life of the Church.

Clearly all of these cannot be addressed, but perhaps we can look at a few. At the outset let it be said that we are not offering solutions. Rather, I am seeking a proper understanding of what those large issues are that affect Church and world and to see if together we can begin to find answers. We often suggest that the world's agenda is forced on the Church. This is not so. It is ours by virtue of who we are.

More than once during the past five years I have written about the mandate that we have for being in the world. Sometimes we talk as if the Church and the world were light years apart and that for the Church to show concern about the world's agenda would be a betrayal of the trust we have been given by the Lord. And yet whenever anyone tries to describe Christ's ministry, it becomes apparent that at every turn the thing that Jesus cares most about is the world.

A short passage in Luke's Gospel (4:16-21) makes this clear.

> And he came to Nazareth where he had been brought up; and as his custom was, he went into the synagogue on the Sabbath day, and stood up to read.
>
> And there was delivered unto him the book of the prophet Isaiah. And when he had opened the book, he found the place where it was written, "The Spirit of the Lord is upon me, because he hath anointed me to preach the gospel to the poor; he hath sent me to heal the brokenhearted, to preach deliverance to the captives, and recovering of sight

to the blind, to set at liberty them that are bruised,
to preach the acceptable year of the Lord."
    And he closed the book, and he gave it again
to the minister, and sat down. And the eyes of all
them that were in the synagogue were fastened on
him.
    And he began to say unto them. This day is
this scripture fulfilled in your ears.

The mission of the Church to the world and for the world
is the unmistakable message of that statement. Interestingly enough, there is nothing here that suggests that the
task of the Messiah (or any of those around Him) is ever
reduced to the point of merely protecting the institution
or anything or anyone who is part of its mission. There is
nothing here to suggest that our energies should be spent
on ourselves.

    We are fond of claiming that our ministry is patterned
after that of our "great high priest," and then we proceed
to set up ways to make that ministry belong exclusively
to the ordained. Or we proceed to look inward at those
things that benefit us or serve the needs of the household
of faith.

    Again, I would not be misunderstood: we need to pay
attention to the household of faith, or else we may lose
that of which we are clearly the stewards. However, our
efforts to protect, to circumscribe, or limit do not fit well
the ministry of the Messiah. After all, when we call
ourselves the Body of Christ, we are claiming for ourselves
a messianic mission. The Church's work is outlined by
the Messiah's calling to be the anointed one of God, sent
by God into the world to announce good news: to deliver
those imprisoned, to open doors for them; to give sight to
those who cannot see; to release the broken and helpless;
to proclaim the year of the Lord's favor.

All of these concerns are messianic, of the Messiah, whose life we are and whose priesthood and ministry we share. They are to be found outside, as well as inside, and they define that point at which Church and the world come together and hold a shared agenda.

The last line of the scriptural passage from Isaiah or, if you will, the messianic mandate is this: "And he began to say to them, this day is this scripture fulfilled in your ears." This may be the most difficult part for us, and it is also the most disturbing. Isaiah has defined the Messiah. The Messiah is imbued with the Spirit, he is sent because he is anointed. Isaiah has also defined the messianic ministry. Jesus reads the lesson, rolls up the scroll, and accepts the whole package and (at least very strongly) suggests that he is that person: filled with the spirit, anointed and sent to carry out the messianic mandate. A very disturbing statement for them and for us, or at least it ought to be.

During the recent past the response of church people to the vast changes that have shaken society has been to demand peace and stability in the community of faith. The anger produced by the South Bend General Convention and the upheavals related to the birth of the General Convention Special Programs threatened what is often considered to be the normal stance of the Church. The various movements and the violent activities of the late 1960s and early 1970s caused all people in our society to long for a more peaceful time and somehow Christians were convinced that the Church would lead them back to that time.

There was and remains great confusion about the peace of which the Church speaks so frequently. In the view of many, change is related to strife, and strife is seen as disturbing the peace. We Christians need to remind ourselves that when Jesus said, "This day is this scripture fulfilled in your ears," he was disturbing the Roman Peace. In quoting the words of the prophet Isaiah, he was reminding the Hebrew people that the Messiah always disturbs the peace. If the Messiah confronts political and social institutions, if he speaks good news to the poor, if he delivers those in prison, or if he opens the eyes of the blind, or calls for freedom for the broken victims, then he necessarily disturbs the peace.

The Church, like its Lord, must stand firmly at that point where the Church and the world meet, and the Church must address the issues of the day, not necessarily as having solutions, but as a body of concerned people who together with other citizens, seek solutions to the large problems of our time.

The Church must address the enormous problems confronting the Christian family in an atmosphere where commitment is limited and divorce is easy. Whenever a marriage is begun in the Church, the Church needs to make every effort to support that marriage and the family it creates. I shall ask the Council to establish a Commission on Marriage and Family Life in order that we may begin now seeking new ways to be helpful.

We continue to writhe and suffer from the racism of our past, and while we have made great strides toward freedom for all, we are not there yet; and we note that there are those who would lead us into that jungle again. The Church must stand against such efforts, must use its resources to prevent such a return, and must further carefully search out racism inside and have it dealt with.

There is still a great fear in this city and all over the land. We have become prisoners in our homes, and night-time in our cities reveals block after block of empty, unpeopled streets. Now the facts are these: this city will never be among the safest in the nation…unless we all seek to destroy those forces that continue to make crime possible. It is not enough to point the finger at the criminal justice system, the media, or the schools. It won't do to talk about television violence or the sexual revolution unless we are prepared to get at the truth, unless we find out what is in fact happening and why. In matters of the causes of crime, the adjudication of cases and the punishments meted out, the Church has a part to play and ought to be there.

Like it or not, the sexual revolution will continue. The gay community will continue to make demands, and while I am willing to address each case individually as I recently have, it will become increasingly necessary to develop a policy that grows out of thoughtful and compassionate concern without denigrating or destroying the Church.

Public and private education, likewise, pose enormous problems. The Anglican Church has been in the education business for four hundred years. Can we serve the larger community on matters of education? I think we can.

Then, there is peace itself. This is the hardest and most elusive. Peace is of God, and each time we have tried to establish it, we have ended in a Babel of sound and strife. The first thing to say is this: So long as there are people, peace will be elusive. So long as there is injustice, hunger, racial or national pride, and hate, peace will be impossible. So long as there are greedy men and women, the Church must act not as the agent of peace, but as the Messiah. The result will be disruption.

I indicated earlier I have no solution to these vast problems. There are no simple solutions and possibly few answers. However, Christian responsibility demands that we join with all the concerned peoples of the world in search of answers. Christians cannot afford the luxury of exclusivism. If we are to be taken seriously in proclaiming the Kingdom, then we must support the search. And if it moves us into controversial waters, then we must walk with our brothers and sisters so long as the means employed are consonant with our faith.

It is my belief that of all the many sects, denominations, and communions that comprise modern day Christianity, the Episcopal Church is in a unique position to stand at that junction where Church and World meet. Any careful look at our own nation reveals the impact of the Anglican Compromise upon our social and political lives. That compromise suggests the cohabitation of widely divergent views in one community. Together we seek the truth—the truth as received by the church as revealed and the non-church community as discovered. But it isn't necessary for Christians to suppose that truth revealed means truth immediately comprehended. If that were the case, then we should long ago have discovered a way to make real the mandate of the Gospel.

Empowered with the Spirit, prepared to seek answers together, ready to love and trust one another, we can become leaders in producing the kind of world which the Church, anointed one of God, is dedicated to ushering in. It will be a world in which peace is both preached and lived; where prisoners are delivered; the sick are truly cared for; and those that are bruised are set at liberty.

Empowered with the Spirit, we pray that the day will come for us when we hear Jesus say, "Today this scripture has been fulfilled in your hearing." Amen.

*John Walker was instrumental in organizing the Interfaith
Conference of Metropolitan Washington, serving as its first
president. When twenty-nine leaders of Protestant churches,
the Roman Catholic Archdiocese of Washington, two Islamic
groups, three Jewish organizations, and three Eastern Orthodox communions met in December 1977 at the Cathedral College
of Preachers on Mount St. Alban, Bishop Walker was asked to
address the summit conference.*

*In the speech, Walker refers to "the Hanafi siege," an inci-
dent in which sectarian Muslims led by Abdul Hamaas Khalis
captured and held hostage three Washington, D.C. buildings
filled with Jews. It was one in a series of international crises
played out in the nation's capital late in the summer of 1977,
just before Walker took his seat as Diocesan Bishop.*

This meeting begins to fulfill a hope which I have had for
a long time—that the leaders of the interfaith community,
the inter-religious community of the Greater Washington
area, would come together for dialogue and concerted
action.

I hasten to point out that this is not a private dream
of mine alone. Others in this room have expressed similar
hopes. Besides, some of us here today are veterans in
interfaith cooperation in Washington, especially involving members of our Protestant, Catholic, and Jewish
communities, and currently are so involved in some
specific areas of concern. As the Reverend [Doctor Ernest]
Gibson (of the Council of Churches of Greater Washington) stated in his letter calling us to this meeting, "The
entire interfaith community of Protestant, Catholic,
Orthodox, Jewish, Islamic, and other faith bodies of the
nation's capital, can be a far more significant resource in
this community—especially, if at critical times and in
critical areas, we all are able to speak and act together."

We have been asked as the leaders of our religious communities to work together today to identify community and other issues and concerns which we share in common, and to begin the development of an interfaith vehicle to address these issues and concerns.

For my part, I do not believe we need to apologize for having such an exclusive meeting today; that is, involving only those as close as is possible to the top of the decision making authority of our respective bodies. As you know, we're very accustomed to making decisions and actions based upon the advice and information of our staffs. Often we find ourselves in the position of authorizing or implementing things with which we've had very little involvement. In some cases, that is fine. But the activity which we embark upon today must not fall in that category. An interfaith vehicle through which we leaders will work together has got to be something which we've thought up ourselves; and we've got to struggle with the issues, and give thought to how such an entity must be structured to work for us. That is why I so welcome this opportunity today.

I have been asked to get our thinking started by sharing with you some ideas I have for the goals of an interfaith entity and how I would see it operate. Based upon the introductory remarks made by each of you at the beginning of the meeting, any one of us could have undertaken this task.

I see four basic objectives for us as interfaith leaders, which an interfaith vehicle would help us to accomplish:

The first objective is communication between us. For the sake of knowing more about each other and sharing our concerns and our faith with each other, not merely in times of crisis, but on some regular basis. I realize our schedules are busy ones, but a few times a year, we could come together—perhaps around a conference format—to look together at some particular community concern, or better still, to foster mutual understanding of the ways and faith of the religious communities we represent. I believe that such experiences will lead us naturally into closer bonds of fellowship, and will strengthen us to work together as we pursue other objectives.

A second objective for us is to be a unified moral force and voice in this community in times of crisis. In some sense, the urban community is always in crisis. But, as you know, we face some pretty drastic and traumatic situations sometimes when a unified religious voice might be extremely helpful. I am thinking particularly of the time of the Hanafi siege. As it stands, the various religious traditions did play their part in easing tension and suffering and in the resolution of the situation as well. But I often thought of how much more could have been done had we all—now in this room—been standing, and praying, and working together. Crises, by definition, are unpredictable so I can't identify specific ones. But other community calamities, riots, pestilence—I think we need to be prepared always to share our faith and resources and to do works of mercy in times of crisis.

A third objective is to be an ongoing force in this community for the social and moral transformation of our society. I said before, that in some senses the urban scene is always in crisis. I'm certain there is no one in this room who would deny it. In Washington and its Maryland and Virginia suburbs, is some of the worst poverty in this country. Here there are citizens, and many who are not citizens, who are hungry and destitute, jobless and in despair. Our young people are afflicted by the scourge of drugs which make them crazy enough to kill—even to kill their parents. Drugs are no respecters of persons. The addict is white, black, young, old, poor, rich, middle-class; Catholic, Jewish, Protestant, Islamic, and Orthodox.

In spite of all the talk about urban redevelopment, a decent home is out of the reach of too many of our citizens, and our aged people are exploited. Although greatly reduced in recent years, crime has not abandoned the streets of our nation's capital. And, in the face of all of these mounting problems and signs of decay, our city government still does not have effective authority to address the problems. The capacity of our communities in the Greater Washington area to address problems effectively and regionally is weak.

The religious community of this area, specifically its leadership, needs first to become familiar with these problems, which all of our people face. We also need to learn more about the systems of our society where the decisions get made, which have such a profound impact on our people's lives. And we need to be able to stand together in support of the systems that promote the well-being of all of our citizens, and stand together in judgment against those which do not. We need to be able to propose legislation, if need be, and to pool our resources for some direct services. We need to come together and develop common cause and common voice, unembarrassed by the great and positive influence we will have in all spheres of community life.

Finally, a fourth objective would be for us, the Interfaith Community of Greater Washington, to be a sign, a visible witness to the Oneness of all the peoples of this community—and of this earth—under the Fatherhood of God. This is a Holy Cause upon which we embark, my friends. We come together from our perspective, because of political and social concerns, because of economic considerations, because of many good causes and reasons.

But in and through these concerns, the All Merciful God calls us out of our various traditions and cultures to accomplish a greater purpose, to unify this broken and divided world.

In the Washington area, race prejudice, inter-religious animosity...none of these are things of the past. And because we dwell in the nation's capital, we identify ourselves with the great national and international conflicts of our age: with troubles in the Middle East, in Northern Ireland, in Southern Africa, and elsewhere. What a fantastic witness if we in this room would be open to one another, would struggle together to overcome our own prejudices, would purposely crumble the walls that divide our faith communities so that we might pray together, and yes, worship together.

When we, standing together under the protection of the God of Abraham, Isaac, and Jacob, and of all people, and inspired by the voice of the ancient patriarchs and prophets, the Cross of Christ, the witness of Muhammad, and great teachers in all times, then we will be a force, a powerful force for good in this greater Washington area. And nothing will overcome it.

Throughout the Church's history, the position of Canon had been the provenance of senior priests serving the Bishop in the Cathedral or of prominent diocesan clergy. In 1983 John Walker installed the first lay people to serve as members of the Washington National Cathedral's Chapter, or governing body. In this sermon delivered at their installation, Bishop Walker links worship, service, and sacrifice and shows these ideas to be the hallmarks of ministry for all Christians.

St. Paul writes in his epistle to the Romans "I appeal to you therefore by the mercies of God to present your body as a living sacrifice wholly and acceptable to God which is your spiritual worship." In another translation of that same passage, the words read thusly: "I beseech you therefore by the mercies of God that you present your bodies as a living sacrifice wholly and acceptable to God which is your reasonable service."

There are three elements in these first verses of that twelfth chapter of this great Epistle to the Romans that are of concern to us in our worship of service and sacrifice. St. Paul goes to great pains in this epistle (as he does in others) to offer some clear definition of what this Church, this Christian life, this body of Christ, if you will, is going to be like—what it will look like and how it will behave.

St. Paul is well aware of the history and background out of which many of these new Roman Christians came, especially those who began their spiritual journey as members of the Jewish community of faith. They came out of a background of service and worship and sacrifice. Sacrifice for them began as the presentation at the altar of animals and doves. But inasmuch as our Lord Christ became for us the final and the great sacrifice, St. Paul knows that something more is expected from the Church.

We are not expected simply to offer animal sacrifice at the altar. And obviously we cannot re-enact perfectly the complete sacrifice that our Lord himself made for us when he went to the cross. But we are called upon by St. Paul to respond to what the Lord has done for us by making a sacrifice of our own—to offer our lives, our bodies, our minds, our spirits, not as a sacrifice of death, but rather as a living sacrifice unto God; giving as it were, of our time, our talents, our resources…giving of all that God has given to us to serve our fellow men and women. That is indeed what St. Paul called our reasonable, our rational service.

But if that were all, it would not suffice. The Bible's words here do not do justice to St. Paul's revelation. We no longer translate Romans 12:1 as speaking about spiritual as opposed to rational service, as if we were to choose between serving God spiritually with our hearts, or rationally with our minds. Our faculties are too intertwined for that to be the case. St. Paul speaks of our spiritual worship, for God made a body and breathed into it the Spirit, the breath of life, and we became living beings. So St. Paul calls upon us to serve God with our body, in all of its forms and all of its functions and all of its activities. We have our bodies by the mercy of God, and by the mercy of God our bodies live.

But, also, we offer back to him that deeper quality of Spirit which God gave to us in the first place, that quality of existence that gives us life and mobility and the ability to act. All that we offer, too, as a part of this living sacrifice unto God. Thus our "reasonable service" is a giving of self—of body and of spirit, of the whole person—in worship and in service to Almighty God, and in service to other human beings.

This Cathedral Church of St. Peter and St. Paul can be seen in these three categories of worship, of service, and of sacrifice. When asked what the mission of this Cathedral is, this is what we might well respond.

The chief mission of this Cathedral is to worship God. It's the thing that we do most of the time. It is, I daresay, very probably the thing that we do best. All day long every day there are services of one kind or another going on in this place. The thousands of tourists who go through this place on a daily basis find herein those services that they might attend, for we are constantly in the mode of worship.

But worship can also be translated as service, service to God in the form of worship, service to God in terms of the actions we take to lift up our fellow men and women, actions that call people to dignity, and actions that recognize their worth before God. Whenever we cry out in the advocacy for those who suffer, we are doing service to God. When we serve others, we are offering that service to God as an act of worship. We do this as a sacrificial offering, not by slaying an animal on our behalf, but by offering our lives in their totality to others. We sacrifice ourselves, with all the brokenness we bring and with all the redemption God has given us through his son Jesus Christ.

It is this essential ministry that forms the business of the Cathedral Chapter. The Chapter is called upon to set policies for this Cathedral Church, but it sets those policies within the framework of worship, service, and sacrifice. And if we do not do that, then we do not carry out the will of those who founded this place as they set out our purpose here as set forth in the charter of this Cathedral.

The Canons and the Staff who work in this place everyday are caught up daily offering their lives (and the lives of all of us together) to God and to God's people. In acts of sacrifice and worship, here they offer God their reasonable service to the Cathedral family, to those who worship here, and to those who never climb up this hill but stand outside in need of service, crying out for the work that Christ has called us to perform.

To sacrifice, serve, and worship. It is for these purposes that we install members of the Cathedral Chapter. It is for these purposes that we name Canons and bring them to their stalls and place them therein. But also there is something else about which we must be concerned, something else that St. Paul points to again and again in the twelfth chapter of the Epistle to the Romans and in all of his writings: that somehow or other, by the power and grace that God gives to us, we must behave in a way that becomes who and what we are.

Always, we seek when we are away from this Cathedral and we gather in places where people know that we come from this Cathedral to present a life that is worthy of this place. For we would have people look at us and see this Cathedral and say that from the Washington National Cathedral only comes the best. Ah, but that is so arrogant, is it not, for us to suppose that in the frail bodies that we have we can be seen as the best of anything? But by the power of God through the grace of Christ, we are enabled to be what otherwise we would not be able to be, namely, transformed—transformed through prayer, transformed through the renewing of our minds, transformed by our worship—so that somehow or other we may communicate to those outside that we are indeed followers of Christ, that we are indeed ministers of reconciliation, that we are indeed those who seek to perform the will of God here and wherever we go.

This ministry to which we are called, this ministry in which we are engaged, in acts of worship and service both here and beyond these walls into the community outside, this ministry is not merely that of those who work in this place, not simply of ordained ministers but of lay ministers as well. Thus, for the first time we have designated that some lay members of this Cathedral Staff should be named Canons of this Cathedral. For their work and their ministry is every bit as important as the ministry of those of us who are ordained. Nor is it limited to those who bear the title Canon. Rather, every person who works here—clergy or lay, paid or volunteer—is called upon at all times and in all places to remember whose name and sign they bear, whose ministry it is to which they are called, whose purposes they serve by being a part of this Cathedral's life.

By the grace of God we have named and installed these persons as members of the Chapter and as Canons of this Cathedral, and we are called upon to set an example for the Church and for the world: to be diligent in our work, to be without guile and pride, to reflect the unity and diversity that is ours as members of this Cathedral community, and most of all, always to act in love so that the love of Christ which fills this place and fills us and transforms our lives may be mediated through us to those with whom we come into contact.

This is our purpose. This is our goal. And with the help and prayers of all of you who join with us in this ministry, we will be able to perform the same, and with St. Paul to say that we are indeed transformed by the love of Christ into persons who are worthy to stand in this place in worship, in service and in sacrifice. That is the ministry to which he calls the whole Church from day to day. Amen.

Chapter 2

The Episcopal Church Welcomes You

Neither let the son of the stranger, that hath joined himself to the LORD, *speak, saying, "The* LORD *hath utterly separated me from his people."*—Isaiah 56:3

It was just after the Second World War when the first red, white, and blue signs began to appear in front of Episcopal Churches across the United States, each one proclaiming beneath the Church's shield, "The Episcopal Church Welcomes You." It was, in one of those odd convergences of history, about the same time that John Walker began his journey toward the Episcopal Church. Through the years he was welcomed into the Church and its most powerful offices. He made it his mission to see that others received a similar welcome, regardless of their race, gender, or sexual orientation.

Walker received his first welcome to the Episcopal Church in Detroit in the fall of 1947 as a student at Wayne State University. Drawn by the worship and social action ministry of the Diocese of Michigan's Cathedral Church of St. Paul (and the generous friendship and financial support of its Dean), Walker before long was on his way to the Old South. By the early 1950s, he had successfully integrated Virginia Seminary. In 1957, he was welcomed by St. Paul's School in Concord, New Hampshire. The Washington National Cathedral welcomed him as its second African-American canon, and in the fullness of time, he became the Diocese of Washington's first black diocesan bishop. He was the second black diocesan bishop in the history of the Church in the United States. He nearly became the Presiding Bishop of the Episcopal Church.

Walker's predecessor as Canon Missioner at the Cathedral, John Melville Burgess, was the American Church's first African-American bishop with jurisdiction, having been seated as Bishop of Massachusetts in 1971. Like Walker, Burgess had served his diocese as bishop suffragan for several years prior to his election as diocesan. The office of Suffragan, or assistant, bishop proved an invaluable training ground, stepping-stone, and platform from which to open people's hearts and minds to the possibility of an African-American bishop having authority over a predominantly white diocese.

Such a recitation of historical firsts is just the kind of exercise that John Walker would find unnecessary. For a man whose life had been shaped by the realities of race in American history, who had been a black pioneer in some of the most traditionally white institutions in the country—John Walker was personally unaffected by the complex racial politics of the Unites States in the late twentieth century. It was something he never let define him.

An act of will? A quirk of personality? A spiritual grace? Publicly, at least, he never cared to speculate. John Walker was always more interested in living for the future than from the past—not that he could ever resist analyzing a problem historically, or ever act unaware of the internal geography of faith whose contours were shaped by his own life experience. Yet somehow, as the Rt. Rev. Richard Emrich realized when he sent the reluctant postulant to integrate Virginia Seminary in 1951, John Walker encountered opposition without ever having learned to hate the oppressor. "It has to be you, John," the Bishop of Michigan told him.

By the time Walker came to Alexandria, Virginia to begin his formal preparation for priesthood, he was well acquainted with racism. As he described it in a series of autobiographical lectures, it was an awareness that did not emerge until his adolescence. Walker's early life was spent in a multi-ethnic Detroit neighborhood surrounded by a family whose faith seemed to be a determined shield against the injustice regularly visited upon them. Not long after he was born, the Walkers had been run out of Barnesville, Georgia. The hot-tempered American Indian that he was, Joseph Walker stormed north with his family after he popped off at the mouth one too many times to the 'good old boys' of Barnesville. The story was known, but not discussed. In much the same way, everyone knew that John had been given Thomas as his middle name in honor of an uncle who had been lynched, probably for hitting a white man, but it was not a subject of family conversation.

As the innocence of childhood gave way to dancing and dating, the stakes were raised, and John Walker's friends began to separate and go their separate ways. World War II began; boys went off to die in far-off lands. But in the south, German prisoners of war were allowed to eat in cafeterias that were closed to African-American GIs. And in Detroit, where the machines of war rolled endless off assembly lines, racial tensions brought on by the need for wartime workers were about to erupt in flames.

In Detroit in the early 1940s, there was full employment but no place for workers to live. (The homeless formed long lines at street corner newsstands hours before the papers arrived, hopeful to be the first to read any new classified ads for housing.) There was plenty of overtime pay but no place to spend it. Everything worth buying was rationed and in short supply. In just a decade, the number of blacks living in Detroit had doubled. Black factory workers, recruited from the rural south, found to their dismay that prejudice and bigotry did not stop at the Mason-Dixon Line. Everything was crowded.

Throughout 1941 and 1942, incidents multiplied as blacks and whites clashed over housing, working arrangements, and public accommodation. In the summer of 1943, during thirty-six hours of rioting, cars were torched, property was looted or destroyed, 1,800 people were arrested, and thirty-four people died (25 of them black; 17 of those at hands of Detroit police.) On the way home from school, John Walker passed by flaming cars. Fear of further violence cancelled his high school graduation.

Later, when he came to Virginia Seminary there were challenges inside and out. Most of his fellow seminarians were welcoming. He remembered being scared. He didn't want to go. After he got there, he said he practically had to be dragged from the campus by his friends to join them at carefully-selected local parishes.

In 1952, when John Walker wanted to have lunch out with his friends, he had exactly two choices. He was forbidden by law from eating with white classmates in most of the Washington area's restaurants. When they tested a couple of other establishments, they were threatened with fines and jail. Across the Potomac, though, they could climb up Wisconsin Avenue in the District of Columbia to break bread. They found a place, in the shadow of a huge half-built Church, where everyone was welcome. Thirty years later, John Walker still welcomed friends to eat with him in that same restaurant. He really had never dreamed that he would some day look down on it, and the city, from the highest spot in the nation's Capital.

Along the way, Walker was swept up by the tidal wave of racial awareness sweeping through the Episcopal Church. Like so many of his generation, the conflicts of the Civil Rights Movement were central in the formation of his priestly ministry. He served as the rector of a white, French-Canadian congregation in Detroit, marched in Atlanta, prayed with Martin Luther King, Jr., and watched the Black Panthers move onto the political scene. In July 1967, he visited relatives in Detroit with his young family, in the first year of his ministry at the National Cathedral. Days later, the city was in flames—and this time there was no shortage of gasoline to fuel the fire. Forty three people died. He warned that it would happen next in Washington. He counseled Episcopalians to act fast, out of love. If they couldn't summon love, then at least, he suggested, they should be motivated by enlightened self-interest.

It was a rallying cry being heard throughout the Church as the 1960s ended, and John Walker was uniquely positioned to deliver the message. As the national crisis loomed, Walker saw it coming in New Hampshire, where he had made it possible for St. Paul's school to welcome black students into its community, but where he felt increasingly isolated from Black America. He arrived in Washington in 1967 as the crisis deepened in the nation's capital. His sermons from 1967–1969 at the National Cathedral capture the urgency and anxiety over the relationship between the whiter power structure and the realities of life for most black Americans.

Bishop Walker preached on the sin of racism many times over the years, worked for the adoption of a national holiday to celebrate the life of Dr. King, spoke at countless memorial services, and argued that the Episcopal Church's General Convention should meet in Arizona in spite of the fact the state did not so honor the slain civil rights leader. (The General Convention did go on to meet in Phoenix in 1991, two years after Walker's death.) He formed diocesan commissions on racial reconciliation, moved behind the scenes to open doors for black clergy, and stood as living proof that black bishops could work effectively with largely white dioceses.

For all that, John Walker realized that the problem of racism was as intractable as ever. In his lifetime he saw many fundamental changes in the way the church and the world dealt with African-Americans. He watched as black professionals multiplied and rose to the top of their respective professions. He witnessed the death of "Jim Crow" laws and attitudes. Yet, in a letter to a young black schoolgirl from Massachusetts, Bishop Walker could agree with the Rev. Jesse Jackson that most blacks were no better off in 1984 than they were in 1943. He would not have been surprised by a 1994 initiative by the Episcopal Church to combat "the sin of racism" with a resolution adopted by the General Convention. He had been nonplussed, after all, when one parishioner asked him, shortly after his election as Bishop Coadjutor, why he didn't just go back and take care of his own people. Bishop Walker remembered smiling and saying in reply, "I thought we were all God's people, ma'am."

Just as it did in American life, the civil rights movement in the Church led to a wider call for other minority groups to have their place at the table as well. John Walker was on the forefront of arguing for their inclusion as well.

He found himself, for example, in the thick of the battle over the ordination of women to the priesthood during the mid-1970s. With his superior, the Rt. Rev. William Creighton, then Bishop of Washington, Walker was an outspoken advocate for women's ordination. He worked locally and nationally to persuade often-skeptical Church leaders that the power of tradition could never outweigh the biblical and moral imperative for inclusion. He publicly and in the strongest terms criticized Presiding Bishop John Allin for his opposition to women celebrating the Eucharist.

Nevertheless, Walker was determined to work within the system, a determination that brought him into conflict with many of the very women whose access to the Church's ministry he so strongly advocated. He counseled patience in a way that offended those who felt they had been patient long enough. He actively worked to dissuade the irregular ordination of eleven female deacons to the priesthood in Philadelphia in 1974. When the Church began its inquiry into the possibility of disciplining the bishops who conducted the ordinations, Walker was one of three bishops empanelled to determine if the allegations against the ordaining bishops would (if proved) constitute a violation of church law. He decided in the affirmative, and helped select a Board of Inquiry to determine whether or not the bishops should stand trial. Those bishops did not stand trial, but their colleagues ruled the ordinations to be invalid insofar as they violated the Church's canons for the process of ordaining persons to the priesthood.

In perhaps the most poignant incident of that tumultuous time, Walker blessed but would not ordain The Rev. Allison Palmer to the priesthood in an ordination rite that took on the character of a funeral. The service proceeded as set forth in the Book of Common Prayer until the point the bishop would normally lay his hands on the ordinand and call on the Holy Spirit to bestow the grace of ordination to priesthood. Walker halted to make a statement. He drew parallels between his own life and the barriers faced by women called to be priests in the Church. He sympathized with their agony. He made it clear that he was committed to opening the ministry of Christ to all people. He expressed his hope that one day soon women would serve as priests and bishops in the Church. Then he took the Rev. Deacon Palmer's face into his hands, blessed her, and watched her walk away into a side chapel of St. Columba's Church in Northwest Washington.

Walker's position was difficult for many to understand. One of the so-named Philadelphia Eleven wrote to accuse him of complicity with his brother bishops in effectively blocking women's ordination for the sake of "collegiality." However, Walker's stance was more complex than an endorsement of canonical understanding among Church patriarchs. On the contrary, his conclusion had been drawn after wide-ranging consultation and serious, painful, personal spiritual reflection.

In a letter to the bishops planning the Philadelphia ordinations, written just days before the ceremony took place, Walker questioned the men's motives, the institutional validity of their intended action, and the possibility that an irregular ordination would "[cripple] and [hinder]...the goal of full participation of women in the ministry of the Church for a long time to come." He wrote,

> I do believe that post-resurrection Christianity demands the oneness of God's people and that this must be reflected in the life of the Church. I believe further that this will not be so for the person in the pew until it is fully reflected in the (ordained)

ministry of the Church. I believe in and am fully committed to the ordination of women. I believe that at some point the step must be taken, but I would hope that the women might show (and we with them) a little of the patience of Blacks as the struggle becomes difficult. I have always been convinced that sometimes we must force change by breaking the law or laws but only after all legal means to redress grievances have been exhausted. I hardly think that the first legislative attempt and failure constitutes an exhaustion of all legal means.

With such logic, Walker staked out for himself a middle path between love and justice, between mercy and judgment, between priesthood and prophetic condemnation. He did not claim it was the only way. He recognized that it was possible for others to offer against it a logical opposition. But, as he wrote to one such opponent, "having thought a great deal, and prayed long" he made up his mind and "remain[ed] convinced that I could not then do otherwise."

The day came when Bishop Walker fulfilled his promise and ordained a woman to the priesthood. His deployment officers worked gently but relentlessly to open doors for women priests to serve parishes in the diocese of Washington. He installed the first women rectors of the diocese, including Jane Holmes Dixon, who would someday follow him as Bishop Suffragan of Washington. At her installation he prophetically affirmed her gifts, and told the congregation of St. Philip's, Laurel, Maryland that when women bishops came, she would be among the first. He was a principal at the ordination of Barbara Harris, Bishop Suffragan of Massachusetts, who *was* the first.

John worked tirelessly, creatively, quietly, reflectively, and insistently to create a community where everyone was welcome. He took issue with those who argued that the growing welcome offered by the Episcopal Church was responsible for a decline in numbers. His analysis was, as always, more historical and more sophisticated than that. He believed that people left the Church because it had been so slow to match the reality of its action with the profession of its faith. The epidemic he diagnosed was not one of modernism, but one of sinfulness, of people and nations seeking instant gratification and great power without sacrifice.

The battles John Walker fought did not end. Racism and sexism continue to infect the Church. Other battles, just emerging as his ministry drew toward a close, were looming. He lived long enough to establish the first full-time chaplaincy for the victims of AIDS, but not to see the still-emerging landscape of gay priests and bishops and the questions about same-sex unions that vex the Church today. Exactly how he would navigate the current crisis is a matter for speculation. The dance between his conscience, his bedrock convictions, and the pastoral circumstances involved would be complex.

But the broad outlines of John Walker's perspective are clear, and they were constant throughout his ministry. In the winter of 1954, a white man from the deep south and a southern-born black man from Detroit wrote a Church History paper entitled, "The Separation of God's People: The Problem of Racial Prejudice in the Episcopal Church." It is filled with the usual puffery of seminarians and the didactic nonsense of academic research. And yet buried in the requirements for a thesis in Church History lies the heart of what John Walker understood to be the nature of humankind, the meaning of the Gospel, and the mission of the Church.

With regard to the problem of prejudice...we are called to witness to the unity of human life in God.

Jesus Christ has overcome our ultimate separation from God, and it is the Holy Spirit which is continually overcoming our separation from other members of God's family.

The Christian answer to the problem of prejudice is that the Holy Spirit and the Church as the saved and saving community overcome our separation, loneliness, and isolation. The proper witness of the Church is to the unity of human life in God, and to the oneness of God's people. Not that racial prejudice is eradicated or removed, but that knowing that ultimately nothing can destroy our unity with Christ, we can live with our prejudices and see them continually transformed by the Holy Spirit. The destructive effects of prejudice on ourselves and on others is now made powerless...

Our course is given to us. We may differ in strategy and timing, but that we must labor to end the separation of God's people on every level...there can be no disagreement.

The problem of race, as John Walker saw it, was not rooted in the sociology of poverty nor politics of discrimination. The solution to racism was not creative social change and increased educational opportunity. All those things were for him merely symptoms of sickness and signs of health. Whether as seminarian, pastor, canon, or bishop, Walker saw deeper, understanding that human sinfulness lay at the heart of the separation that made blacks, or women, or homosexuals unwelcome.

That made the problem more intractable than ever. Yet strangely enough, this analysis gave John Walker the hope that shone throughout his ministry, for he always believed, as he wrote in 1954, that, "We are secure in Him who overcame all things for us." He was as sure as St. Paul, whom he quoted to end his senior thesis:

...[T]hat neither death, nor life, nor angels, nor principalities, nor things present, nor things to come, nor powers, nor height, nor depth, nor anything else in all creation, will be able to separate us from the love of God which is in Jesus Christ our Lord (Romans 8:37-39).

This 1963 baccalaureate sermon, delivered to the graduating class of Tilton School, a New Hampshire preparatory school, probably represents John Walker's first public statement on the problem of race in the United States. His rhetoric skillfully employs the theme of patience, drawing in an audience poised to challenge his prophetic realization that America's failure to deal equitably with "the Negro" would soon lead to a "hot and bloody" future.

Late in the speech Walker considers the not-so subtle racism of the press, prone to ignore accomplished African-Americans while at the same time sensationalizing the eccentric and the scandalous. He refers to Bishop C. M. "Sweet Daddy" Grace, founder of the charismatic United House of Prayer for All People, and U.S. Representative Adam Clayton Powell, Harlem's flamboyant congressman for almost a quarter of century. Both men advanced the cause of civil and economic rights for blacks in a tempestuous era; both men's colorful personalities and questionable ethics led them, in the eyes of many, to disgrace.

I am grateful to you for inviting me to come to Tilton to deliver this Baccalaureate sermon. My subject this morning is one which I have attempted to avoid for the six years that I have been in New Hampshire. The lesson read from the Gospel according to St. Luke suggests the subject. I regret the necessity of speaking to you on this subject, but in view of recent developments in our troubled land, I believe that it is crucial that I discuss with you the racial problem in the U.S. I am sure you do not want to hear a sermon on this subject, but before you doze off or sink into your Sunday sermon reverie, allow me a minute of your time in patience. I think I can ask this in view of the fact that most Americans are asking the Negro to be patient after 344 years of one of the most extraordinary examples of patience in the history of man. But whether or not you are patient enough to hear, I shall continue knocking, for this concerns all of us deeply, the issue is whether we will choose integrity or death or, as a well known psychologist has put it, whether we will "Love or Perish."

The Lesson read for today deals with two problems applicable to our situation. First there is the importunate man who continues to knock, followed by the story of the Divided House. In the first instance the man finally gives his friend the bread not because of friendship but because he persists in knocking at an ungodly hour, and the man gives in to shut him up. In the second part of the lesson, St. Luke confronts us with a world that is divided. It is a world without integrity where men degrade themselves by preaching one doctrine and practicing another. It is a world ripe for destruction because it has no guts and it has no conviction. It is a world that would live by law, but seeks to circumvent its own law. Finally, it is a world into which Grace comes but cannot be exalted because it refuses to belong exclusively to one people.

From the time of Jesus (and even before) until now, men have looked at their own special worlds and have contrasted them to those of the pagan or barbarian and said. "It can't happen here. We are too advanced. We have evolved well beyond that stage." But history indicates that it did happen "here." It happened in the Religious wars in England, France, and Germany. The world looks back in horror at the Spanish Inquisition and the burnings in much of Europe; the beheadings and hangings in France, England, and Salem. And certainly by the 1840s we Americans were all convinced "It couldn't happen here." But the U.S. Civil War came; the economic crimes of imperialistic capitalism came and ended in World War I and II, and since then, ever smaller segments of the "civilized world" are able to say, "It can't happen here."

We would answer that we have been conducting a noble experiment in Brotherhood, and that we are all agreed on this—thus, we believe that we Americans can escape the accusation of living in a divided house. We delude ourselves and say (with a touch of self-congratulatory pride) that it hasn't really happened and probably never will happen here. Of course this isn't so. Was there any essential difference between what Red China did to Tibet and the new American nation that pushed across the Appalachians and drove on to the Pacific? Is there any actual difference, except in scale, between the German treatment of undesirables and our treatment of Japanese Americans in the 1940s? Of course, we might rationalize for ourselves an answer, but would any impartial witness be convinced?

It has been said that we Americans are a schizophrenic people with a split personality. We have a psychotic fear of something we can't quite define, but we act as though it were indeed very real—even to the extent that we legislate against it with little or no regard for what such fearful legislation does to the foundational idea of our social covenant: that all men are equal before God and the law. So great is this fear that Christianity has been largely helpless against it, and it has almost succeeded in swallowing the church. To say the very least, it has rendered the Church so ineffectual that an increasingly large number of people do not want to be identified with this trembling, frightened body of Christ.

A hundred years ago Abraham Lincoln paraphrased this Gospel theme with regard to slavery and its continued existence in the U.S.: "A House divided against itself cannot stand." Lincoln was convinced that this nation could not continue to exist half-slave and half-free. But a very large group of our citizens were convinced that it could so exist, that we could claim to be the champions of democracy and suppress our minorities at the same time. Is it unfair to say that from that time, and before, this nation has lived a long and very big lie?

We have convinced ourselves that our crimes against humanity are different from those of other nations, that somehow Birmingham or The University of Mississippi are different from South Africa or Hungary or East Berlin. We seek justification by saying that Martin Luther King, Jr. is an opportunist, when he is simply importunate. We say the Negro is not yet ready for full citizenship because he has not done enough with what little freedom he has had. "Let him prove himself," we say. The problem is, of course, that no matter how great may be the Negro's progress, it is never enough—never enough.

I have recently re-read some of the many articles that were written concerning "brainwashing" in Russia and Communist China, and about our reaction to this phenomenon. Do educated Americans really believe that this phenomenon is peculiar to Russia or China? We brainwash our citizens just as effectively. We simply use different methods.

Until very recently there has been little or no mention of American Negroes in many of our high school history books. The G. W. Carvers, Marian Andersons, Leontyne Prices, James Baldwins are usually ignored. It is as if they don't exist. On the other hand, the Clayton Powells, Daddy Graces and those who degrade the Negro are carefully written up (certainly in the press), practices that seem designed to continue the myth of white superiority.

Recently a national magazine ran a series on crime in the nation's Capital. By using all the right statistical data, the study "proved" that the Negro is responsible for most of the crimes of violence there, and by implication, elsewhere in the U.S. Strangely there was no mention of the factors which have produced the rebellious, vengeful, hating Negro.

I could go on.

Perhaps you think these matters don't matter much for you in this lovely, isolated community. But this service is a reminder to you that your time here is short. You will soon be back in the world of political and social reality, and you will be asked to make decisions on this very issue—either as Christians, or simply as Americans. I believe it is our duty to warn you about the world out there. It is likely to be both hot and bloody. My appeal to you today is to seek integrity—but not integrity merely. I implore you to seek integrity that is anchored with a deep sense of love for your fellowman.

The era of *noblesse oblige*, of paternalism toward our minorities, has passed. All over the world, suppressed men and women are on the move. If we continue to protect our old lies, we may see ourselves swallowed up in the very fires of change which we helped to build. If the Church is to wield the kind of influence it ought to have, then you must recall it to the basic principles of its own Jesus of Nazareth. If the nation is to survive in the kind of world we live in, you must resist our national lie with all the power you have. For just as persons who live in unreality need to be hospitalized, so too, a nation which persists (as we have) in practicing bigotry must be quarantined and left in isolation away from all the nations of the world who are truly interested in the freedom of humankind.

The issue is integrity or death: you must love, or you will perish. A house divided against itself cannot stand.

On September 17, 1967, Canon Walker delivered this sermon at the National Cathedral, just a year after he began his ministry there. It is a remarkable piece of oratory, combining historical insight, scriptural interpretation, and a timeless analysis of power. In a few pages, John Walker both indicts and interprets blacks and whites for each other, offering a balanced critique of an increasingly polarized discussion of race in the late 1960s. The costly price of reconciliation to which the title refers is echoed in a passing reference to eggs and milk: the exorbitant price-gouging to which Walker refers would put the value of a dozen eggs at $10 in 2004, with a gallon of milk ringing-up for about $25.00.

The Churches have been asked to observe today as Refugee Sunday, and while this sermon which I have prepared is not specifically about refugees, its subject lends itself to that matter because it concerns itself with all of those in this land or in other lands who might be called the dispossessed. If I were asked to give a title to this sermon, I would call it "The Power and the Price." The New Testament Lesson read this morning, St. Mark 10:35-45, is on the face of it concerned with the matter of true greatness, but it is also about power. St. Mark begins with a story of James and John who come to Jesus and ask to sit on his right hand and on his left in his kingdom. Now it is well known that those who sit on the right and left of a king hold the greatest power after the king himself. It would appear then that they are not simply asking to be near Jesus, but rather to be given great power. Presumably from these positions of power they could assist in the judgment of their peers and the rest of mankind. It is for this reason that the other disciples were angry with them.

Before Jesus answers their question; indeed, even before he hears it—he himself asks the most crucial question of all: "What do you want?" This is of great importance, for Jesus promises in the passion prayer that if they (and the emphasis here is on the plural) ask anything in His name, He will grant it. So James and John should be careful of what they ask. They put the question and Jesus answers by saying "You do not know what you ask. There is always a price to pay—are you able (not are you willing, but are you able) to pay that price? To bring in my kingdom I must drink a bitter cup and be baptized in a painful death. Can you pay that price?"

In their naiveté, they answer yes. For they do not realize that they cannot be good enough even to deserve the title of disciples without the grace of God, and those prized positions in the kingdom are not simply given to those who strive and succeed in some earthly sense…not given to those who simply happen to be liked…but are given to those who by God's grace are able to be faithful.

Saint Mark then takes up the question of greatness and he reverses its normal conditions. In the human situation, then and now, greatness is too often measured in terms of the number of servants one possesses and the degree of one's material power over others. In the kingdom Jesus has come to bring about, this will not be the case. The king or the rich man who wields economic, social, or political power over others will not necessarily inherit the mantle of greatness. But the man who sees himself as the servant, if you will, as the slave of his fellows, he shall be accounted the greatest in the kingdom of Christ.

This is a difficult concept for men because it asks them to achieve greatness in life and then to subdue their ego and to slough off the pride and the glory in order that they might serve others. Indeed, the mission of the Christ is to be the ideal servant of God. Thus, He whom we worship is not seen as a king; a symbol of political power, but as King and slave to those whom He loved and for whom He paid the ultimate price.

The questions "What do you want?" and "Who is the greatest among us?" are very pertinent even in our time. Our nation was born with great promise. It was to be a haven for the dispossessed—for those without political, economic, or religious freedom. It would be a land where all men, and eventually women, would be equal. Justice would be every man's birthright, not just for those born into the right families, or those of high education and great wealth.

But this promise, like every promise of man's, was watered down. Somewhere in the power struggles of the 19th and 20th centuries it almost disappeared. The arrogance of power was very real in the United States when Andrew Jackson entered the White House and initiated a new era in democracy. The economic and political rulers asked "What do they want?" and they, the people, answered in electing Andrew Jackson, "We want to participate in the power which guides this nation." But like James and John they naively assumed that they were able to pay the price; they naively assumed that the grace was automatically theirs by which they might pay the price and the price was, of course, to subdue their own egotistic passions and help bring about the fulfillment of the American dream. Historians would argue that the Jacksonians moved us along the road to democratic fulfillment, and perhaps this is true. But like their predecessors, they began to default on the payments and found themselves victims of the arrogance of power.

The Civil War came and went, and we entered the great period of industrialization. Still the dispossessed cried out for justice and for the right to participate. The form of the struggle was one of strife between labor and management. The American worker was no longer satisfied with the crumbs from the rich man's table, and that revolution was fought and won. But the dream was not realized for it simply created a new class of dispossessed. The workers, like the Jacksonians—like James and John, assumed the ability to pay the price and assumed that the grace was theirs by virtue of their position. The price was high, for it was nothing less than the sharing of economic security with all others. Every American has the right to the pursuit of happiness. But that pursuit is meaningless unless he has the means to achieve some measure of economic security.

In these times we still seek the fulfillment of the dream. We have just come through a summer of strife in our cities and more than once in the past three-and-a-half months I have heard the cry raised, "What do they want?" and *they* (in this case) are the American Negroes. But before we attempt to answer this one, let us recall that part of the promise of this nation was that our rulers would not lord it over us, and by rulers I don't mean just those in government, but the whole social, economic, and political power structure of our land.

The question "What do you want?" was, in the mouth of Jesus, a penetrating one designed to help James and John see the absurdity of their request. In the mouth of the power elite; whether it be the Virginia dynasty, the Jacksonian democrats, those who represent management and labor, or simply the white American who lords it over his black brothers, the question becomes synonymous with the naked arrogance of the powerful.

Every white American who asks "What do they want?" presupposes that he has the right to ask such a question and presupposes that the Negro has no right to make demands. When he says, "We have given and given, and we aren't going to give anymore," he presupposes that it is a question of his right to give or to withhold the

American dream. In so speaking, he reveals the great poverty of his understanding of the American system.

But arrogance is not the possession of white men alone. It is St. Mark that Emerson quotes when he has God ask, "What do you want?" Then Emerson has God continue, "Take it and pay for it." "I'll take it, all right," says the revolutionary young Negro. "This is what I expect, and you'd better not expect me to pay. I have already paid enough." He rightly indicts the white power structures. He rightly cries out, not for condescending grants but for what is the right of every American. But then he spoils the whole thing by arrogantly demanding that every man agree with his methods. If the dream is worth anything, then we must all, black and white together, be prepared to pay the full price for its fulfillment.

If we would solve the problem within the context of the American experience, the Negro must continue to pay the price of patience and understanding—assuming responsibility at every step. James and John were called in the end to drink the cup of suffering and to accept the baptism of death; namely, martyrdom. In the struggle to realize every man's dream of political justice, of economic security, and social acceptance many have died in this nation as well, and perhaps more will yet die.

Most of us, though, will be called upon to make a different kind of sacrifice. For some the cup of suffering and the baptism of death will take a different form. It all depends on how we answer the crucial question "What do you want?"

Do we want racial peace in our land? The price is high. There must be a reconstruction of our aims and policies. Perhaps this will mean the writing of new laws. The whole nation must be willing to help the Negro to rise on the economic ladder even as white Americans have been aided by such means as the Homestead Act, tax rebates, and the protective tariff. The great wealth of this nation must be shared with this large group of the dispossessed. It certainly includes the right and means to education; given, not condescendingly as we might give in to a child, but by releasing from our grasp that which is rightly the birthright of every citizen of this land.

Protection must be available at every level to Negroes who wish to exercise their right to vote, for no man should face losing his job because he has exercised this cardinal right. The price for racial peace today is often in terms of suffering in our hate-filled communities. It leads often to ostracism in our churches and alienation from the majority view and from the majority group. It has already meant this for many all over this land. Further, it might mean to stand against those who hate, against the interests in every community that benefit from division and segregation. Make no mistake about it, there are those who do. In the recent riots in Detroit it became necessary for the city to pass laws to protect those who had lost everything, for there were human scavengers who charged as much as $1.00 a quart for milk and $2.00 for a dozen eggs.

The price we must pay is to stand against every person or organization that peddles hate, whether they are on the side of white power or black power. The arrogance of power for these men suggests that the community or the nation will be better under their views than under their predecessors or their would-be successors. They would have us believe that abusive power is somehow related to color. Personally, I am no more anxious to live under the naked hate of black power than I am to continue under the more subtle hate of the white power structure.

The answer finally must rest in the recognition of who we are and on what great promise our nation was founded.

We are not a nation either by declaration or by charter in which men lord it over each other, but rather one in which freedom, equality, justice, education, economic security, and social pride are held in common by every man. What do we want as a people? To live in peace? Then let us take it. We have the power. But if we take it, we must all pay the price. Do we also have the grace necessary to pay what it will cost to be truly free?

In this 1984 appreciation of Dr. Martin Luther King, Jr., Bishop Walker introduces his topic by referring to Paul Tillich. Tillich, perhaps the most influential systematic theologian of his era, spent most of his career at Union Seminary in New York, a subway ride uptown from Trinity Church Wall Street where this speech was delivered. In it, John Walker offers a stinging critique of the American "melting pot." Walker views the Great American Melting Pot as a sham, nothing more than a subterfuge designed to re-create all outsiders in the image of the white mainstream. Its only utility, he argues, was that it served as a foil against which King developed his prophetic call to authentic racial equality.

"It all goes back to Eden," thus the professor of Systematic Theology began his lecture on the finer points of Paul Tillich's theology. The time was 1949-50, and a visiting lecturer was about to launch into a discourse of Tillich's understanding of the human condition. In the course of that lecture he would use such phases as "a state of dreaming innocence," "the ground of being," and "rebellion against God." All of these ideas have, in the succeeding years, become familiar phrases to us all.

It did all begin in Eden, not only our belief in Creation, but the hopes and dreams of all humanity (men and women) from that day until now. In Eden, Adam and Eve were in the womb of God, protected from danger, unaware of life, experiencing the joy of pure being and of being pure. It was a life in which all was known and yet all was unknown. Known were the joy of bird song, the companionship of other life forms, and the beauty of nature. Unknown were hate, confusion, anger, conflict, and despair—all the negatives of existence in the world. It was the perfect Utopia; one man, one woman, without true knowledge of life beyond or outside the womb, living in perfect harmony with God. It was indeed a state of dreaming innocence.

The expulsion from the Garden brought Adam and Eve face to face with hostile reality. They were forced to fend for themselves. They had to compete for food with other beings that inhabited the earth. Eventually, they would find themselves competing with and against other beings like themselves. Conflict would develop; danger lurked behind every tree; instruments were made to slay animals for food and clothing; others to fell trees to provide shelter. Later, these would become instruments of protection and defense.

Precisely when the dream began we cannot be certain. (But, I suspect, it was early on). At some point Adam and Eve stopped in their tracks, looked around and asked. "What are we doing here, naked, cold, and hungry? We are worried about our life, for there are animals who would eat us and strangers who would kill us. Why did we ever anger God so that he expelled us from His Garden? If only we could go back!" But, of course, as you and I know well, you can never go back to innocence, never return to the womb. We can only move ahead, using the dream as a guide, seeking as best we can, to bring the dream to reality.

Whether it is Abraham, Isaac and Jacob, or Moses and Aaron; whether it is David and Solomon, or Isaiah and Jeremiah, the dream has persisted for a new Utopia, a new Jerusalem. History is strewn with the partial and occasional fulfillment of the dream or the wreckage of its disintegration.

But whether wrecked or fulfilled, the dream goes on. We hear it in Virginia in the voice of Patrick Henry: "Give me liberty or give me death!" or in the words of Abraham Lincoln: "Fourscore and seven years ago, our fathers brought forth, on this continent, a new nation, conceived in liberty, and dedicated to the proposition that all men are created equal"; or in the fireside chat of Franklin D. Roosevelt: "The only thing we have to fear is, fear itself"; or Martin Luther King, Jr., "I have a dream." Whatever words express it, whose ever lips or pen may be its author, the dream is always the same: it is of "...a new heaven and new earth."

When Martin read these words, every hearer knew that he believed them. But more than that, we came away believing ourselves that he was certain that the promise of America, if realized, would be the dream fulfilled. Later, in the harsh light of reality, we would reassess our thinking. Some would say, "Nah. He's got the thing all wrong. The dream can't happen until we get rid of all foreign elements." Or we might be left to say, "The dream is beautiful but, but it can never be realized—not even here in America, for we are sinful people locked into original sin from which we cannot escape." Others would call Martin a communist; he called for equality that extended outward to include economic opportunity. In his vision of America, everyone would have an equal chance. The nation would be color blind, because you have a fair race if one has had a leg amputated, or is hampered by the color of his skin.

What recourse does the man of color have? Do you peel off his skin, or bleach out all the color? Or do you abandon the dream, fire up the melting pot, and toss in anyone who's willing?

Martin knew (as we all know) that the melting pot was a cop out. We can't build a nation conceived in the idea of liberty and justice for all. That notion creates too many problems. William Penn may have come up with a holy experiment but it won't fly in Philadelphia let alone Manhattan or Richmond or Atlanta. The solution? It must be the melting pot, we thought. Dump them all into a cauldron: the English, the Dutch, the French; add religion, language, and every other aspect of culture; stir in politics, economics, land-property rights, the vote; mix well, bring to a boil and let it simmer; pour mixture in to a mold; cool until the blend is set. Now…out should pop the new man, the new American. Now, we were sure, we could make the dream of liberty and justice, peace and prosperity for all, come true. Now, all Americans will be the same: white, blond, blue-eyed, manly in appearance.

But this is no advance at all. It merely makes us a new Europe, and there's little good in that. In western Europe they were all white, and they all destroyed each other anyway. For years they had one—repeat one—religion, and they still fought over who held the keys to the kingdom. They had a single system of government, and they still killed each other for the right to rule. Even in those places where a single language existed, the distrust was enormous, and internecine warfare was the order of the day. How could we possibly believe that homogeneity would produce an atmosphere in which peace, prosperity, liberty, justice, and security could thrive and grow? There could be no excitement there.

What happens in this scenario to the "other," to the native American, to the Africans brought here by force, to other people of color who have come? The same thing always happens. The other must be kept apart, must not be allowed to spoil the stew. You must isolate native Americans, keep blacks enslaved as workers (or send them back to Africa), exclude people of color, and keep out everyone else who bears any mark of inferiority, by establishing immigration controls.

That's what happened in the so-called melting pot. Slavery for African-Americans continued even after it was ended, transformed into the powerful Jim Crow. Native Americans lived and died on reservations. Orientals were excluded. Jews and Catholics were suspect. The idea of a great American Melting Pot was a dismal failure. When seen within the context of the Declaration of Independence, the Revolution and the subsequent Constitution, it makes liars of us all. It destroyed all interconnectedness between our holy documents (that is, what we said about ourselves) and the practice of democracy. Unless the dream is in fact dead, the Melting Pot's only possible utility is the chance that from its flagrant failure would eventually rise a new Prophet in our midst. A prophet who would force us to look at ourselves; who would shame us into honoring our holy documents, cause us to display them as the folklore of a forgotten race of dreamers, or to scrap them altogether.

Martin was such a prophet. He marched, he preached, and he went to jail. He was single-minded in his devotion to the dream. Each year we honor him and rightly so. But part of that honorarium must be an annual assessment of how far we have traveled along the road that leads to the dream's fulfillment. Do our laws recently passed, does our economic activity, does our public behavior help to build the new Jerusalem?

And don't hide behind the idea that the "new Jerusalem" has only eschatological reality, that St. John's dream is imagined about the second coming, that it is somehow a myth about the next life. The new Jerusalem that Martin talked about—indeed, that our Lord himself spoke of—was not just to be read eschatologically, rather it was about the reversal of the way we see and do things. In St. Luke's gospel there is a summary:

> But I tell you who hear me; Love your enemies, do
> good to those who hate you, bless those who curse

you, pray for those who mistreat you. If someone strikes you on one cheek turn to them the other also. If someone takes your cloak, do not stop him from taking your tunic. Give to everyone who asks you and if anyone takes what belongs to you, do not demand it back. Do to others as you would have them do to you.

Logical? From a human point of view, no. Possible? Yes—Martin's life taught us that.

Chapter 3

On This Rock

And when the builders laid the foundation of the temple of the
Lord, they set the priests in their apparel with trumpets...
to praise the Lord.—Ezra 3:10

Deep beneath the great building, anchored on eleven
feet of solid concrete, buried under half a million tons of
Indiana limestone, lies the granite foundation stone of the
Cathedral Church of St. Peter and St. Paul. In its heart lies
a smaller stone from Bethlehem on which are inscribed
immortal words from the Gospel of John: "The Word
became flesh and dwelt among us." In 1907, President
Theodore Roosevelt, the Bishop of London, and sixty-two
bishops of the Episcopal Church and of the Anglican
Communion across four continents watched as it was laid
into place with high hopes and great fanfare. The excitement of a new diocese and a new century, the emergence
of the United States as world power, the optimism born
of prosperity and innovation, the flowering of a belief that
Episcopalians were destined to be the nation's spiritual
leaders of the world to come—all this and more had swept
Bishop Saterlee and his financial backers to launch an
audacious plan to build a huge gothic church from which
they could keep watch over the capital.

Sadly, within a year, Bishop Saterlee was dead. Within
a decade, World War I had set the stage for the bloodiest
fifty years the world has ever known; in just a little over

twenty years, the country's good times would crash around the feet of the bankers who had helped the first Bishop of Washington pay for architects and masons. Yet through it all, the Washington Cathedral kept rising. From 1912 on, services were held in its Bethlehem Chapel, whose altar lies directly above the Foundation Stone. Course by course the building grew: chapels, transepts, altars, choir. In 1964 bells rang for the first time from the Gloria in Excelsis tower high above the crossing, and the Rev. Michael Hamilton joined the cathedral staff, charged with "relating the Cathedral to the world."

Canon Hamilton was soon looking for an assistant. He thought naturally of his friend and seminary colleague John Walker. In July 1965 (while he was on sabbatical from his work at St. Paul's School, teaching in Uganda), Walker received a letter from Hamilton inviting him to apply. A year later, Walker was the first one interviewed. He was offered the job on the spot. It took just five years for Walker to win the hearts and minds of the Cathedral community, and it became clear to the diocese that he was logical choice to serve as its bishop suffragan. His increased visibility on his weekly half-hour television show, which began several months before the election, did not hurt his chances, either.

In his annual report to the Dean, Walker wrote:

> I had not suspected in September 1970 that I was entering my fifth and last year as a Canon of Washington Cathedral... I leave the Cathedral itself, though not the community, grateful to have been a part of this place, and grateful for the opportunities it gave me to become deeply involved in the Washington community and thereby developing a new kind of ministry. As Suffragan Bishop I hope to continue to serve this Cathedral Church and to support what it struggles to become—a House of

> Prayer for all people; a symbol of hope for all who
> are without hope, and a sign that faith lives on in
> the human heart and leads men on to produce the
> best of which they are capable.

He would not be gone for long.

As bishop suffragan, Walker watched as Dean Sayre's bold plan for the Cathedral began to take shape around him. Sayre convinced the Cathedral Chapter that the nation's approaching bicentennial presented the perfect opportunity to push construction forward. First came the western façade, then the final stones of the Cathedral's perimeter, and finally the dedication of the completed nave. It was 1976, the same year John Walker was elected Bishop Coadjutor, designated to succeed Bishop Creighton as the Sixth Bishop of Washington on Creighton's retirement. On July 8, after he finished assisting in the liturgy of a "Service of Reconciliation for All Peoples," Bishop Walker walked between Prince Philip of the United Kingdom and Mrs. Gerald Ford, down the Pilgrim Steps that led from the Great Western Front, just behind the President and the Queen.

When the trumpeters left and the last notes of the carillon had disappeared into the summer air, the nation went back to dealing with its economic troubles, and John Walker soon learned that his cathedral had economic troubles of its own. The year 1977 was a dramatic one on Mt. St. Alban: the new Bishop faced the retirement of longtime St. Albans School headmaster Canon Charles Martin, the impending retirement—after more than a quarter century as Dean—of Francis Sayre, and the surprise of a record $12.5 million construction debt.

In the face of such challenging opportunities, Walker made two bold decisions: he would unify the mission of the Cathedral and diocese by serving as the chief executive officer of both—as bishop and dean; and he would hand to his successor a finished building, debt-free.

He began to restructure Church House (diocesan headquarters) and the Cathedral clergy to fit his vision. He launched fundraising campaigns in the Diocese of Washington and across the nation to retire the debt and finish construction on the Cathedral. Bishop Walker insisted that along with money for building, funds had to be raised simultaneously to continue and expand the Cathedral's programs. His insistence is testimony to the fact that he saw the Cathedral's completion not as a monument but as a key for ministry. As great as was his love for the liturgy and the building that housed it, even greater was his love for people; he knew that every dollar spent on bricks and mortar was a dollar that could not be spent meeting human need.

So John Walker threw himself into a new ministry of fundraising. Drawing on his winsome personality and the extensive network of corporate leaders with whom he had come in contact at St. Paul's School, at Beauvoir, and at St. Albans, Walker hired consultants, encouraged volunteers, and made the overtures toward big money by himself. He relied heavily as well on the groundwork laid by the corporate fundraising skills of Charles Perry, his Provost. Summing up Walker's accomplishment, William Tully, then Rector of St. Columba's, the diocese's largest parish church, wrote, "It is hard to know whether anyone else, placed in the same time and circumstances, would have, or could have, envisioned and made possible the completion of the Cathedral."

Given the timetable of cathedral building, things moved quickly. On July 18, 1977, construction was suspended for lack of funds. In January 1978, a capital campaign was announced. By September 29, 1980, construction had resumed. In April 1983, the Cathedral's front towers began to rise above roof level. On January 25, 1984, the external construction debt was retired. By 1987, bronze entrance gates and the last of the 106 gargoyles had been installed to spray runoff rainwater away from the St. Peter tower. In 1989, as landscaping began for the Cathedral's West Front, plans were laid for a year-long celebration of consecration and dedication. On August 31, 1989, the final installment of internal construction debt was repaid to the Cathedral's operating fund.

The building was essentially finished and completely paid for. The coffers were full and visitation was at record levels. A full program staff was in place. The hardest work over, a great celebration was scheduled for Michaelmas, September 29, 1989, exactly 82 years after the first stone had been laid. A crowd gathered for the festivities surrounding the raising of the last finial of the Phillips pinnacle on the northwest corner of the St. Peter tower. Shortly after noon, the huge stone was blessed and soon soared into the heavens toward its place, some thirty stories above the crowd.

As the stonemasons finished sealing it into place, John Walker died.

Cathedral Provost Charles Perry, writing in *Cathedral Age*, was not the only one who saw "[w]hat a cruel irony it was that Bishop Walker died" as the Cathedral began "the celebration of the fulfillment of his dream." The Bishop had been scheduled to preside at the day's dedication. News of his death spread quietly through the cathedral community, who kept up a brave face while entertaining the crowds who had come for the celebration. At Evensong, Walker's death was announced publicly. A trombone choir played reflectively, and the people gathered found a different meaning than the liturgist had planned when they recessed singing, "Crown Him with Many Crowns."

The following Thursday, amid the necessary and much greater pomp and ceremony of symphonies and bishops—but not without the plaintive gospel melodies of his childhood, too—John Thomas Walker's funeral was held in the Cathedral he loved. Five thousand people came to mourn him. There were leaders of church and state and not a few ex-convicts. Male and female, Jew and gentile, rich and poor, black and white gathered beneath the embossed gothic arches and wept openly for the man who had embodied the enormous building and what it had come to stand for under him.

He had somehow summed it up, all of it: the Chapter, schools, guilds, artists and musicians, the volunteers. He was a master of governance (*"Almighty and everliving God, source of all wisdom and understanding, teach us in all things to seek first your honor and glory; guide us to perceive what is right, and grant us the courage and will to pursue it..."*); and education (*"Almighty God, who gives us power to reason, experiment, and discover, grant us to know that which is worth knowing, to love that which is worth loving, and above all to search out and do what is well-pleasing in your sight..."*); a poet and patron of liturgical art and lover of all things holy (*"We thank you Lord for sacred places burnished by wings of holiness, for shrines consecrated by prayer, and lives suffused with Thy quiet peace; be ever present with your servants who seek through art and music to perfect the praises offered by your people: grant them...glimpses of your beauty, and make them worthy at length to behold it unveiled for evermore..."*); a wholly hospitable man (*"O God who gives thy Holy Spirit without measure to those who prepare for him a dwelling place: make us worthy temples of your presence, that we may joyfully and rightly welcome…your guests").*

In the great building's heart lies the slate box containing the earthly remains of its Sixth Bishop and Fifth Dean, John Thomas Walker. He rests on solid rock, anchored in death as he was in life to the foundational belief that as God had loved him, so he had been called to love, the Word made flesh.

The psalm applies:

O how amiable are thy dwellings, thou Lord of hosts! Blessed are they that dwell in thy house: they will be always praising Thee.

Canon John Walker gave this address, "Washington Cathedral and the Inner City," to a meeting of the National Cathedral Association in 1967. In that year he began what would become a thirty-year relationship with the now century-old organization founded to support and promote the Cathedral's mission and ministry. (Today, the NCA boasts over 12,000 members representing every state in the Union.) During the final phase of construction, fundraising by the NCA provided a bay of the Cathedral, the Pilgrim Observation Gallery, and a conference center above the nave. The last stone erected, on the first anniversary of Bishop Walker's death, was the finial of the National Cathedral Association pinnacle on the St. Paul (south) tower.

Although he had served the Cathedral less than a year, Walker clearly had already developed an intuitive grasp of the institution's unique character as he explained its religious, denominational, social, political, and national roles. In this speech he foreshadows his own ministry as a bridge between Washington's power elite who ran the country and the ordinary folk who kept the capital running. Essentially, Walker argues that insofar as the Cathedral is concerned, all politics are local.

Any discussion of the local thrust of Washington Cathedral is meaningless except as seen alongside its broader thrust—if you will, its relation to national problems. As you are well aware, the Cathedral is not a parish church, nor should it be seen simply as another diocesan Cathedral. There is, I suspect, little argument that this Cathedral must have a special function in relation to national problems. If for no other reason than that it has a symbolic relationship to the other famous Hill in the nation's capital, it must assume a role in this city that takes it beyond the ecclesiastical boundaries of its relationship to the Diocese of Washington.

This should not be said in any arrogant sense, but simply with the cognizance that this Cathedral is of too grand a design and too bold a conception to belong solely to the Episcopalians or the Episcopal Diocese of Washington. But this does not prevent us from using sparingly, if at all, the title we have assumed of National Cathedral. The Episcopal Church in the United States may rightly ask at which General Convention did the Church give Washington Cathedral this title, and certainly no one else has the right to do this officially.

Having said this, let us now examine our two concerns, the local and national thrust of the Cathedral, to see how these are related. First, let us be absolutely clear that by local we do not mean parish or community church. It is, I think, perfectly clear to us here that we must not confuse the local involvement of the Cathedral with that of a parish or community church. The neighborhood programs entirely appropriate to St. Stephen and the Incarnation, Ascension and St. Agnes, or St. Augustine's Chapel would be quite inappropriate and ill-advised for the Cathedral. By local involvement I mean the involvement of the Cathedral in the projects, causes, and problems that bear upon the life of this city. This need not be financial support but should certainly be (at the very least) moral support and presence.

Briefly, let us examine one or two such problem areas. The crime problem, both adult and juvenile, is a serious one in the District. It is fraught with implications that bear on several other problems in Washington. It is a problem that in large part is related to poverty. Lack of employment, lack of decent housing, the lack of a sense of participation in the great prosperity of this nation is both frustrating and dehumanizing. And inevitably these lead to a disrespect for parental authority, for church authority, and finally, for civic authority.

Secondly, it is related to the whole question of civil rights. There is in this city and across the nation little faith on the part of Negro people in the fairness of the police. Probably every adult Negro male in this land, including this speaker, has, at one time or another, had an unhappy experience with the police, whether or not there was even any reason for suspicion. The certainty in the Negro community that police are not only unfair, but that some are not above brutality, leads to a further disrespect for the representatives of the law and a refusal to assist the police in even elementary ways.

There is no doubt in my mind that the Cathedral must identify itself with this problem and those related to it and must lend whatever resources it has and can toward the discovery of a solution. A beginning has been made. Recently I was invited to attend a two-day conference on the Report of the President's Commission on Crime in the District of Columbia. The conference was sponsored by Georgetown University through its Institute of Criminal Law and Procedure in cooperation with the Consortium of Universities of the Washington Metropolitan Area. It is interesting to note that while several clergymen were present, they were representing either federal or civic agencies concerned with the problem, the National Association for the Advancement of Colored People, the United Poverty Organization, the Washington Urban League, and the D. C. Parole Board. The Cathedral was the *only* church or religious institution participating as a religious institution.

The conference revealed the tremendous need for someone outside the political, social, legal, and economic structures who might be able to talk to both the representatives of the power structures and of the "people of the city." For two days these groups, and the representatives of the "people of the city," talked *at* each other but never seemed to make contact. Is this an area where the Cathedral can serve the community? I think it is.

There are unbelievable problems related to health, education, and welfare and to housing and urban development. From these I have chosen education as another example of possible Cathedral involvement. Again we note how this problem proliferates. Like crime, it is related to poverty, unemployment, slum living, and civil rights. In Washington an overwhelming majority of the students are Negro. Many white people in this area send their children to private schools. This fact both attests to and increases the poor quality of education available in the District. Even those who manage to complete high school are not well equipped to go on or to demand anything like decent employment. Can any of you imagine what this does to a person's incentive to learn? The drop-out rate increases, and with employment levels low for the drop-out, we turn out more and more potential crime problems. Recently I have been invited to join the Committee for Community Action in Public Education (CCAPE). Again, I believe this to be a way in which the Cathedral can legitimately get involved and lead itself to the pursuit of a solution to an important community problem.

We began by talking about the relationship between the Cathedral's local and national thrust. Let us look at this problem in the light of the problem areas examined. The kind of local, inner-city involvement I have mentioned here is significant because it does not stop with itself. It leads in two directions. First, any involvement in problems pertaining to crime or education in the District of Columbia leads inevitably to confrontation with the power structure of Washington, which is by definition national.

Secondly, it leads to greater possibilities for ecumenical cooperation since most religious bodies in the District are involved in these matters.

Further, it can be stated categorically that this activity in no way threatens or duplicates the programs and concerns of local parish and community churches. In investigating possible areas of concern I have sought to abide by the concept of what this Cathedral should be doing. By this investigation I am convinced that the Cathedral must make contact with the day-to-day problems of the District of Columbia. We seek the goodwill and economic support of this community, and we must, therefore, make contact with it. I am aware that we do, in fact, do this. I have simply offered here the way in which I am trying to deepen the thrust and the contact and to broaden the Cathedral's ministry on local and national levels. For always in this city, the big issues that appear to be local are always and inevitably national issues, national problems, and national concerns.

After construction of the Cathedral re-commenced on a "pay-as-you-go" basis in 1980, John Walker presided as Dean over many special dedication ceremonies for a variety of specific pieces of stone and glass that were joined together to complete the building. In this 1981 sermon, Bishop Walker dedicated the West Nave cross. He drew on his knowledge of American history to connect the cathedral's past with its mission as defined by his episcopacy. The Cross was given to memorialize long-time Dean of the Cathedral Francis Sayre, from whom Walker had inherited a completed nave.

In 1897 as our country stood on the brink of the Spanish-American War, the Rt. Rev. Henry Y. Satterlee, the first Bishop of the new Diocese of Washington, called for the raising of a Cross of Peace as the first monument to be built on the newly obtained Cathedral lands. After a year of work on the project, there was a gathering here with a large number of people (including the President of the United States) to witness the raising of the Peace Cross looking out over the city of Washington. The act signaled the beginning of an enterprise—the construction of a National Cathedral—which would occupy most of the 20th century. But it signaled more than that, for it set the tone for the meaning and purpose of the National Cathedral.

By its form and through its ministry, the Cathedral would focus attention on its Incarnate Lord, the Prince of Peace. It would, in fact, seek to be in itself a living sign of that life which was dedicated totally to peace. The message is clear throughout the building. Its inscriptions sing out: a House of Prayer for all people. The carved statues from the unfinished Adam to the majestic Christ tell the story of a human pilgrimage—all peoples of the earth seeking a way back to their source of life, searching inwardly and outwardly for that spark of divinity which would reconcile us to God and lead us into peace. The form is the cross; the pilgrimage is the cross; the life, the death, the resurrection, each is seen in the cross and through the cross.

It is a cross of peace, of truth about our life, and about justice in the world. For us, it raises every question of existence and provides the only sensible answers in a world of nonsense. Just as they gathered eighty-odd years ago to raise the Cross of Peace, so we gather today to raise the Cross of Reconciliation. The coming of the Prince of Peace was for no other purpose than this, to reconcile the world to the Father and thereby to reconcile humanity to each other.

Just as peace, that most elusive of all human dreams, would be a permanent concern of this Cathedral, so too would reconciliation, that hard task that has occupied the very center of the Church's ministry for two thousand years. All who come to this place to work or speak must proclaim, by their life and by their words, peace to them that are far off and peace to them that are nigh.

Some will raise questions about the Church's involvement in anti-nuclear, anti-war, and in peace movements and demonstrations as though the Church could reasonably do anything else. Some will say that the Church does not know enough to address such issues. I submit to you that taking a position against war does not reflect a simplistic understanding of the world but rather it demonstrates that the Church which claims to be the Body of Christ, the living word of the Prince of Peace, must in its life and in its every action raise Him up before the world.

In this seventy-fifth year of the life of this Cathedral we will focus our attention on reconciliation. In 1977, four years ago on this the last Saturday in September, I was installed as the Sixth Bishop of Washington. I prayed then that reconciliation might be the mark of my ministry as Bishop. To choose that as the theme for the seventy-fifth celebration is not to abandon the theme of peace; rather, it is certain that peace can only come about as we take the steps that lead to reconciliation.

The failure of humanity to achieve peace is tied to our failure to recognize our need for confession and forgiveness. We commit ghastly crimes against each other both as individuals and as nations and in the end we struggle not to look at our past, not to remember. Thus, as we move forward, we suddenly discover that we are hampered by past sins; by the victim's inability to forget the crimes of the past; or by our inability to confess. In such an atmosphere, reconciliation cannot take place and peace slips away from us again.

In offering this place as a House of Prayer for all people, we are led to say with the psalmist (and let me paraphrase him): 'We acknowledge our transgression and our sin is ever before us.' In that acknowledgment, in that stated confession, we are made ready for reconciliation. No longer do we see ourselves as the wronged and the other as the transgressor, rather we are both together sinner and victim. We have both together erected a dividing wall between us and we are incompetent to knock it down. The wall of which I speak is the wall that separates race from race, male from female. It is the wall on which the burning cross stands, symbol of hate and aggression in communities across our land; it is the wall of apartheid separating and dehumanizing the black and white people of South Africa; it is the wall that prevents peace in Ireland, in Poland, and in El Salvador. It is, if you will, the wall that separates rich from poor, Muslim from Jew,

Protestant from Catholic, and Christian from non-Christian.

Even so, we dare to launch the next period in the life of this Cathedral by raising this Cross, a Cross of Reconciliation. We do so in the firm belief that the God of Abraham, Isaac, and Jacob calls us to this. We do so in the belief that the message of the prophets, the prayer of Muhammad, and the life of Christ all point us to peace and reconciliation. We hear it said again and again that we have to begin somewhere. We invite you to begin with us in our search for reconciliation and peace. Let us not shrink from the discussion of even the most difficult subjects. Let us talk of an end to racial antagonism; let us talk of disarmament openly and without fear; let us pray with the Irish (Protestant and Catholic) in their agony. May we stand against apartheid, against Communism, and against every political and economic system that dehumanizes people.

But more importantly, let us raise up this Cross and this Cathedral to tower above this city to remind us always that our true ministry is not finally against anyone; but rather it is for justice, for truth, and for peace in reconciling love.

In this "House of Prayer for All People" we pray, we preach, and we work to make it a place of meeting, and a place of reconciliation for all of the people of this or any land, so that fear, distrust, and greed for money and power may be overcome by the overwhelming love symbolized and living in this Cross of Reconciliation.

> We thank you Almighty God for the gift of the Cross reminding us of Christ's reconciling love and of his redemption of us. We thank you for this Cathedral built here to your glory and as a remembrance of His most holy life. On this day we do dedicate this

Cross to your glory that it may be to this city and nation a sign of your peace; your final gift to the world. Finally, we thank you for the life and work of Francis Bowes Sayre, Jr., whom we do honor in this gift. Grant unto us, O Lord, the courage and the power to take up the cross and follow Our Lord Christ who lives and reigns with you and the Holy Spirit, one God, now and forever. Amen.

Chapter 4

Shepherd and Bishop of Souls

He shall feed them and he shall be their shepherd.—Ezekiel
34:23

When John Walker's ashes were laid on the High
Altar of his cathedral, beside them on the table was a
shepherd's staff. From one point of view, it was a shocking juxtaposition. Here had been a consummately modern
man, a witness to the vast technological progress of the
twentieth century, now set alongside the ancient tool of a
peasant herdsman. In the silence of five thousand voices
stilled by grief, people listened that October day in vain
for the sounds of a great heart beating for the city—for
John Walker was an urban man, a man who lived and
worked and loved in the busy city streets where a majority of Americans live. And yet the last sacramental
relationship the Bishop could establish between his
body and his people was an essential, almost mythically
pastoral sign: he shared the altar with a shepherd's
primitive stick.

Not many saw the contradiction. The faithful had
grown used to seeing the Bishop of Washington carry his
crozier, the pastoral staff. The staff was the symbol of his
Office and an ensign for his authority over the Diocese of
Washington. It was a reminder also of his responsibility
to take care of his Master's flock. It is an ancient symbol,

drawn from the words of Christ himself, whose ministry it came to represent. It defined John Walker, even in his death, as a pastor to his people.

Shepherd is the metaphor that has always best explained the meaning of ordained Christian ministry. From his earliest days at his grandmother's knee, John Walker had felt the call to be a pastor, to be a leader of God's people. He became a strikingly successful pastor. He was a shepherd whose sheep knew and recognized in his voice the words of someone who knew them intimately, fed them lavishly, prepared a way for them in safety, stood by them when they were in jeopardy, and drew them toward their common Master in unity. Both kings and convicts cherished his counsel, and no matter which one he was listening to, the person left confident that he or she had been fully understood.

He was always teaching, stretching, persuading, gently chiding or encouraging, calling forth the Church to do its slow but vital work of "binding up the wounded, and, without drumbeat or fanfare, offering its life for the lives of the people." He "opened privileged eyes to a world filled with inequity," according to a friend from his St. Paul's days, but always with a "kind, gentle, loving manner." He was closer than a Father to students from that school, changing their lives in ways both "quiet and deep." He was a comforting presence, leaving anyone he met with the feeling that he liked them, as one student wrote, "no matter who I was, what color I was, or what I did." Inmates watched him on TV and hoped to bring their families to "his Church" one day. An employee whom he prepared for confirmation learned from him "to truly love her fellow man, her Church, and God."

Such pastoral ability is as much art as skill, as much gift as preparation. But in addition to the considerable natural gifts John Walker brought to what would eventually become his role as Chief Priest and Pastor, he brought a lifetime of disciplined study and careful self-reflection. Walker was aware of how his life history had shaped him as a person and as a pastor. In a retreat with the clergy of his diocese, the bishop surveyed the stepping stones toward his vocation: the accomplishment and broadening knowledge of high school, the drafting of all his friends for military service in World War II (as the last son, he had been allowed to remain at home), his involvement with and later breaking away from the AME Church, his substitution of political activism for religion in the heady days that followed victory over totalitarianism in Germany and Japan, his entrance into college and Confirmation in the Episcopal Church, and his seminary matriculation.

But the young man whose first real job was as a government librarian would always read his experience through books. Walker relished the written word. He read widely and with great interest. In 1987 following surgery, a bout of malaria left John Walker without the energy to pick up a book. His family and friends knew that he was really sick. He spent much of his long-awaited sabbatical recuperating, but as the time drew near for him to re-engage with the business of the diocese, what he was most excited about was the fact that he had regained his energy and desire to read. It was a disposition that had held since his college days when, sorting through the option for his future, he sought to understand his call to be a pastor by reading books.

The decades in which John Walker came of age and began exploring a vocation in the Church were without a definitive pastoral theology. Early Church Fathers like Gregory and John Chrysostom had devoted a great deal of attention to the meaning and function of pastoral ministry in the Church. The great thinkers of the protestant reformation had developed detailed theologies of ministry, no surprise since they were by and large pastors themselves. By the late 19th century, vast tomes were filled with careful reflection and lengthy exposition on what it meant to be a pastor. However, this accumulated wisdom was not widely available to seminarians forming their pastoral identities in the 1940s and '50s in the United States.

Undaunted, John Walker read across the theological spectrum in the process of gathering the raw material from which he fashioned a very strong pastoral identity. Even before he arrived at Virginia Seminary, Walker had soaked in the works of Stephen Neill, great Bishop of the Church of South India; Sam Shoemaker, was instrumental in founding Alcoholics Anonymous; and Sheldon Hale, of St. Philip's Church in Harlem, the largest Episcopal Church in the United States.

From Neill the young John Walker caught a vision of ecumenical unity, as the Church of South India emerged with the new nation on the subcontinent in 1946, combining Methodists, Presbyterians, and Anglicans into a heretofore unseen denomination that respected the contributions of each faith while forging an unprecedented unity in doctrine, ministry, and worship. From Hale, founder of the Calvary Rescue Mission, the young man bound for seminary learned the power of congregational involvement in the world's social and political affairs.

Yet, the greatest single influence of the emerging ministry of John Walker was probably the prolific work of the Rev. Sam Shoemaker, whose book *Revive Thy Church, Beginning With Me* had a profound effect. Decades later Walker still knew the book well and lived out its philosophy nearly to perfection. Shoemaker was the spiritual advisor and confidant of Bill Wilson, the alcoholic who launched the worldwide Twelve Step Movement that has rescued thousands from the ravages of addiction. Historians of Alcoholics Anonymous credit much of its success to the primary texts that largely reflect the experience and teaching of Sam Shoemaker.

Shoemaker's ideas and methods (for AA and for Christian congregations) involved making "fellowship" a central function. He organized small groups focused on the development of individual church members within the context of developing personal relationships. Shoemaker wrote, "More is likely to happen between two people guidedly talking together than as a result of the average sermon, provided one of those people has had a genuine experience." Shoemaker's words are a road map of Walker's pastoral approach, first as priest and then as bishop.

As pastor, Walker wisely looked to find that "genuine experience" in others, even the youngest of children. When the director of Beauvoir, the Cathedral Foundation's elementary school, chided him for talking over the head of her youngest students, he counseled her that it was his job to help them "rise to understanding." But for those who had to rely on him to bring genuine experience to the pastoral relationship, Walker had a full cup of his own. The two he most readily identified were foundational narratives of his earliest years which he summarized as death and baptism.

For Walker, the deaths of too many family and friends during his childhood gave him painful experiences he would never have chosen. Though an unwilling participant in observing the dance of death in these events, they made his heart a caring and open one, rather than a bitter one. He became an expert in caring for others and in considering ultimate ends. He was forced to answer early the hard questions of pastoral theology: What is the meaning of suffering? How do you die well? What comfort is there in the face of death? Who can help those left behind? What do you say, and when? Where is God when evil seems to win? The answers he found were in the Sacrament of Baptism, a life-affirming Sacrament that had a profound impression on him. He could recall with razor-sharp detail the scene when the singing crowd, swept up into clouds of joyful celebration, watched him plunge beneath the waters and rise to new life in Christ. He drew strength from their affirmation that he belonged with the believers, and that in the community of faith that they represented, the mysterious all-consuming God of love was unveiled for all to see.

"New life in Christ" was the title under which John Walker filed his episcopal ministry, too. His election as bishop in 1971 opened a new range of pastoral opportunity. He took up the shepherd's staff and held it lightly right away. The convention that elected him had been called specifically for that purpose, and he was a leading candidate from the start. On the heels of the unprecedented racial tensions of the late 1960s, the diocese had set out to elect an African-American assistant for Bishop William Creighton whose diocese included all of the District of Columbia, where blacks outnumbered whites by more than 2 to 1. Not much more than twenty years earlier, the ratio had been reversed.

In the first words he spoke following his election, the Bishop-elect spoke of gratitude, humility, and love: "One thing of which I am convinced in my own life is that without the love we have for each other, nothing can be accomplished. Or, indeed, if anything is accomplished without that love, it is not worth very much." He went on, "We began on this road two years ago. We have come to the end of it in one sense, and in another sense, we have only come to its beginning. During that time we have worked together—sometimes it has been in anger, but always, I hope, in love."

As bishop, Walker came into his own as a pastor. His understanding of the bishop's role was clearly shaped by and remained true to the vision set forth by Jose Antonio Ramos, Bishop of Costa Rica, who preached at his Consecration on June 29, 1971. Bishop Ramos envisioned episcopacy in classical terms, as the embodiment of the Apostolate, that line of authority and doctrine that stretches from the living Church back through time until it reaches Christ's own life and teaching.

Bishop Ramos, and the man whose consecration he was interpreting, reached deep into what it meant to be Apostolic (from the Greek *apostellein*, "to send"). They saw themselves as standing not in a line of succession through which passed power and privilege; instead, they saw themselves as missionary bishops—shepherds sent to serve God's people, not to rule over them.

Bishop Ramos linked the pastoral ministry of the bishop to the biblical idea of love:

> Consider the very essence, the very soul, of this apostolate. "As my Father has sent me, even so I send you." This corresponds to 'As my Father has loved me, so I have loved you.' Which is to say that the essence, the soul, of the apostolate, what sets in motion this great missionary sequence that has its origin in the Father; what sets in motion all mission in the Church, starting from the Father and passing through Christ and the apostles, to this day is *agape*, love—the love that gives, the love that

loves, not for some benefit to be obtained for itself but simply for the sake of loving... The very essence, the very soul, of the apostolate is...love.

It was with this charge that John Walker took up his staff and became a bishop in the Church.

Throughout his ministry, the shepherd's staff he carried as a symbol of his office was employed in the love of which Bishop Ramos spoke. The sermon that Walker heard as he prepared to put on his cope and mitre spelled out the sacramental realities of his office in no uncertain terms. "John Walker is to be a servant of the Lord," Bishop Ramos explained, "armed with the staff of a shepherd, of a pastor—a staff that stands for the power of love which gives him the strength to care, to feed, to seek for, to rescue, to lay down his life for those entrusted to him— his flock. He is given a towel and a basin to wash the feet of the brother and to plunge into the depth of human life and dirt; his weapon is the oil that binds the wounds of a broken, hurt, fallen, and sick human world."

Bishop Ramos warned John Walker that his pastoral staff bore witness to the power of love; it was never to be wielded, he insisted, by a pastor in love with power. These words were a warning that Bishop Walker kept as a touchstone of his episcopacy. Over the next fifteen years, Walker would become a powerful man with powerful friends. He sought power, consolidated power, explored the nature of power, and used both the power of his personality and the power of his office effectively. But there is precious little evidence to show that John Walker ever *loved* power.

In his moving reflection written just days after Bishop Walker's death, former Georgetown University President Fr. Timothy Healy wrote in the *Washington Post* of what he called Walker's "secret power": his priesthood. "It is so easy for prelacy in the 20th century to be what it was in the bad old days of the 16th: more princely (in preoccupation if not in style) than priestly." But, Healy continued, "Despite the fleshpots of the world's most powerful capital, [Walker] never yielded to power's blandishments, never yearned after its rewards."

Yet that is not to say that Bishop Walker was reticent to exercise his authority. There were those who found him autocratic and unyielding. He engaged conflict head-on, and having decided on a principled course of action, carried it out in the face of sometimes heated opposition. In an interview given to a Church magazine profiling candidates in advance of the 1985 election of the Church's Presiding Bishop, Walker explained his use of episcopal power.

First, as always, he identified himself as someone dedicated to reconciliation. "But reconciliation," he argued, "does not mean sweeping things under the rug or showing weakness in the face of important issues. It means confronting those issues... It means using all our energy to help people understand why...and to try to convince them of the rightness of what we are about, rather than attempting to browbeat them into submission."

In the midst of controversy with parishioners opposed to the ordination of women priests, Walker wrote to a detractor, "I do not expect you or anyone else to 'bow (your) heads in submission' to any position I may hold. I live with disagreements on a daily basis. If you knew me at all you would know that I welcome advice and counsel that may be counter to my own... I shall not respond further on this matter. All has been said that needs to be said."

To another opponent in the same controversy, from whom Walker had received a vitriolic letter that accused him of holding positions *"contra mundi Anglicani,"* the Bishop clearly exercised the power he most wanted to wield as the shepherd of his flock. "It is my prayer," he wrote, "that your heart may be turned to more loving ways even if we forever disagree on this matter. It is only in the spirit of love that true unity can grow. I invite you into a relationship of Christian love with me and others who disagree with you even as I have with many of your associates. Try it...It is wonderfully cleansing."

The shepherd's staff was used in ancient times to keep the sheep together. The staff that John Walker carried as Bishop of Washington had for him that primary purpose. As he conceptualized pastoral ministry, Walker developed a profound understanding of the bishop as focal point of unity within the Church. This was not a novel understanding; the *episkopos* (Greek for "overseer") has always been a living symbol of the "one, holy, catholic, and apostolic Church" spoken of in the creeds. But for Bishop Walker, the creeds only reflected the words of Jesus, whose dying wish was that his disciples might "be one."

In a 1986 sermon delivered at the consecration of Allen Bartlett as Bishop of Pennsylvania, Walker revealed an even deeper meaning of the bishop's symbolic representation of unity. Unity, he explained, is a fundamental human desire that has been a driving force in the history of philosophy, religion, and politics. In John Walker's mind, this "holy hope for unity" is made flesh in Jesus Christ, signified by the Church (the Body of Christ in the world), and made present in the Church by the bishop's servant ministry.

It was a sobering sermon delivered that cold February day in Philadelphia as Bishop Walker preached. To a festival congregation, gathered to celebrate the accession of its new bishop, Walker drew an honest portrait of an urban world in which the church, because of its own inadequacy, had only a "faint voice":

> Who will respond when we cry for unity? Who will rise up when we ask for sacrifices so that others may live better lives, when the Church has for so long taken the safer path that continues life as it has been—safe in our separation, safe in our view that we are more fortunate than others because we have earned the right to be? Who will respond to our prayers for peace when Christians are so uncertain as to whether to heed the voice of the Prince of Peace or the voice of political leaders? Or worse yet, who will respond when we are silent in the face of evil—silent because we fear that the people will rebuke us? It…were better to fear the rebuke of God for our silence.

He goes on to cite destruction, terrorism, hate, and persecution around the world, then asks, "Must we not fear that judgment will overtake us for our dawdling along the way, for our waste of precious time lost in the centers of pride, arrogance, and vainglory?" And then he relents, "But enough!" and shifts to talk of celebration and thanksgiving. Then, he reminds the man about to receive his own shepherd's staff, "Beware, my brother, of those who would elevate you on high, who would seat you in the company of the mighty, who would dress you in robes of wealth and royalty… You must stand at last before the world clothed only in His protecting love."

God's love was, for John Walker, an all-encompassing, all-protective cloak. Yet he was wise enough to understand that its protection was most available to those who made themselves most vulnerable. Tucked away in his private papers there is a note from a seminary classmate to a young priest lost in depression. Walker seems to be afraid, afraid that his first parish ministry (with a declining parish of white Episcopalians in the rapidly transitioning inner city of Detroit) was a lost cause. Plagued by petty disagreements, constricted by outdated attitudes, rejected by those who would not trust him, Walker turned to his friend for help.

There is talk of vacations planned, support systems to be built, financial assistance to be given. There is reflection on the relationship between personality and priesthood. And there is a timeless observation and some excellent advice, both of which across the years to come, John Walker would take to heart. Look, his friend wrote back, "[L]ove cannot be expected to win out instantly." He concluded with these words: "Live a spell, and love deeply."

At the crisis points of his ministry, when John Walker was himself most vulnerable, he turned again and again to his friend's words. The summer of 1985 was such a time, following a year filled with "pain, sadness, and depression." The Bishop had traveled to South Africa for the enthronement of Archbishop Desmond Tutu as the Primate of the Anglican Church in South Africa, where he "nearly despaired." He returned to face the forced termination of a member of the cathedral staff. The diocesan ordination of deacons was disrupted by a Pro-Life group. Searches were underway for two senior positions in the diocese and Cathedral Foundation.

He would soon be embroiled in the politics of South Africa, and he had become a candidate in the upcoming election to choose the next Presiding Bishop of the Episcopal Church. But what the shepherd and bishop of his flock felt most was love, "known and felt" from his people. What he called on his people to do was "wait on the Lord." It is easy to imagine him standing, staff in hand, reciting the words of John Greenleaf Whittier with which he closed his column that June.

> I know not what the future hath
> of marvel or surprise,
> assured alone that life and death
> God's mercy underlies.
>
> And if my heart and flesh are weak
> to bear an untried pain,
> the bruised reed he will not break,
> but strengthen and sustain.
>
> No offering of my own I have,
> nor works my faith to prove;
> I can but give the gifts he gave,
> and plead his love for love.

In this sermon given on the Sunday before Ash Wednesday 1989, John Walker's compassion shines through, along with his unyielding faith that no evil is great enough to resist the power of love. Bishop Walker refers to the headlines of February 1989, such as an ayatollah's fatwah, or death sentence, against writer Salman Rushdie, and to a spate of violent robberies in the Washington metropolitan area in which a number of young men were killed. Nonetheless, his concern for terrorism and the perils of the modern world seem almost prescient in light of current events.

Poor, Ignorant Children

Our world just now seems to be spinning out of control. Terrorism, which has held hostage our world for much of this century, continues in the Middle East. It has spilled over into European capitals. Ireland is always with us. And here at home terror, like a wild animal, stalks the streets of our cities and towns and invades the once safe place where our children play and study. Each day brings a new list of senseless killings for a jacket, a shirt, a radio box, or a pair of designer sneakers. Our newspapers are filled with stories of violence in families, violence within nations and between nations of the world. Nor are our privileged children exempt. A boy kills his girl in an act of violent loving. Girls must be careful to avoid "date rape." And if all of this is not enough, we now have the makings of a "holy" terrorism in which a government calls for the murder of a novelist because they do not like what he said about their religion.

Everywhere things are breaking up. Old stabilities, old certainties are gone and old laws are no longer applicable. We speak to one another but we do not listen because the words no longer have meaning. Everywhere words are being spoken but there is no understanding. One is reminded of the words of William Butler Yeats in his poem "The Second Coming":

> The blood-dimmed tide is loosed, and everywhere
> The ceremony of innocence is drowned;
> The best lack all conviction, while the worst
> Are full of passionate intensity. (1920)

Last night I sat watching the late news as the head-shaven neo-Nazis paraded and went through their exercises with "passionate intensity," calling for the elimination of "niggers, Jews, and all others who are different from white (Aryan) original Americans." Poor, ignorant, misguided, insecure children, who would destroy all of God's children to guarantee their own position of power. They are so in need of a savior; not a Hitler (or other dictator), not a past head of the KKK, not even a good man or woman, but a true savior come from God.

Against the strident voices of these American assassins who raises a voice; a black here and a Jew there? But against this "passionate intensity," the best seem to "lack all conviction."

Of course, it isn't all bad. There are many with passionate conviction. For example, the mother who wrote to a program sponsor taking him to task for sponsoring a television program in prime time with near pornographic sexual activity. Many have joined with her even against the angry cries of another producer who asked, "How dare she?" What? Mere mortals question the wisdom of every producer? Assume that the views of Christians in our society deserve a hearing in the exchange of civic ideas? The world out there is filled with evil. But as Yeats says in the same poem:

The darkness drops again, but now I know
That twenty centuries of stony sleep
were vexed to nightmare by a rocking cradle.

Is it possible that the child in the manger still has the power to vex a nation; to irritate and provoke it into action; to jolt it into a sense of its own peril? I believe that it is possible. It will, probably, take a little longer, perhaps a stronger jolt.

Lent is a time of jolting, of reminding us of who, in fact, inhabits that cradle. He is a vexer of peoples and nations. He came, not to bring peace, but a sword; he came to stir up the people of God to action before some final denouement struck them.

But he is more than one who merely vexes and confounds. He is also One who transforms the world. The world suffers, but He suffers with us and offers us a path through death and resurrection to true transformation of ourselves and the world. Everything must experience the change that came over him in the transfiguration. Every rock, every tree, every blade of grass, every animal, or dweller in the sea, every bird, every woman, every man must be transformed and made new. The whole creation must become new so as to carry the new life of humankind. Again I turn to W.B. Yeats who writes in his poem, "Easter 1916" about a drunken useless man:

He had done most bitter wrong
To some who are near my heart
Yet I number him in the song;
He, too, has his resigned part
In the casual comedy;
He, too, has been changed in his turn,
Transformed utterly;
A terrible beauty is born.

He includes all creation, even the stone, even the despicable people in the transformation. And who is to bring this about? The child in the cradle who continues to vex the world. The man on the cross who looked down with loving eyes and forgave that world. He who was raised from the dead in majesty and in the mystery of his glorification. He has enclosed us within the circle of his own transfiguration, and as new beings in him we are empowered by the Holy Spirit to change the world. It is by this and only by this that we will be able to slow down the spinning world, and the cycles of hate, terrorism, and disaster.

John Walker often noted that early experiences of death had a profound impact on his self-awareness and his call to ordained ministry. In this address to a symposium of hospice workers in 1980, Bishop Walker explores the experience of three people whom he knew closely, all of whom moved through suffering and death, confident that they were but continuing a pilgrimage — giving back the lives they owed that they might flow deeper and richer in the ocean's flow of God's love. His observations speak to all those who live under death's "unanswered question mark."

In the Midst of Life

When I was in my early teens I had a classmate, a young Cuban boy, a Roman Catholic, who suddenly, at the age of 13, was stricken with cancer. He lived one year and he died. Many of us would go to visit Rene everyday. We watched him grow thinner and thinner until he died. We were told by his parents and by the teachers at school that Rene was almost constantly in pain. I do not recall ever hearing Rene say that he was in pain. He would often ask all of us to read to him from the Psalms and we would do this. He would sometimes even talk about what death meant to him, for he knew he was going to die. We would weep as we listened to Rene because we did not understand what he meant. He talked about eternal life. Whether or not he was simply mouthing words that he had heard within the body of the church or within the family, I don't know. I will never know, but I do know this, that he would often say when we would ask him if he was in pain that it did not hurt very much.

Then there was Martha. Martha was a woman in our neighborhood, who I knew most of my life and with whom I kept in touch with for many years. Martha was sick for most of her life. She had borne too many children; she had lost too many children. But strangely enough, during all of these problem years of her life, her faith deepened. I can remember several groups of children being in her presence and listening to her sing. She would sing the great hymns of the pre-Civil War, slavery days, which she had learned at the feet of her own mother. Somehow or other, when she was singing she had no pain. Or she read scripture.

But maybe the most significant part of it all was that she lived in hope. Not hope of a miracle that she would be relieved of pain and suffering in this world, but she lived in constant hope that she would find a place in eternity. Never sure what that place would be, only certain that it would be there. I recall, on one occasion when her doctor came, and my own mother was present, and the doctor said, "I don't know how she manages to live with the pain that she lives with, but I guess it must be faith." Clearly it was faith in her case. She lived a long life. She left great examples to all that knew her of how to cope with pain and suffering and how to die gracefully and with dignity and in full acceptance of that death.

And there was Bertha, the last one, a friend who I came to know in my twenties. A woman of great strength and great faith. A registered nurse who worked for doctors in the city of Detroit. Who knew that she had terminal cancer and told almost no one. Worked hard for three years and then I remember one day when she came to visit me, at my church, she told me, for the first time, that for three years she had cancer and did not expect to live very long. She went into the hospital, and that time, I discovered that she had gone into the hospital every four months for three years, when the pain would become so great she couldn't bear it outside anymore.

On the day of her death I went to the hospital to see her. I was there at the time of her death. She was in intense pain for a few moments and then she said, "Excuse me. There is one person I haven't said goodbye to." She left her bed and she went to see a small boy who also had terminal cancer. She said a prayer with him and she returned to her room and she died within the hour. She found her spiritual life in serving other people in a hospital. The doctors said that she was a tremendous person when it came to helping others face up to the terminal illnesses that they have. Whenever any person was in depression or weeping, Bertha would come into the room and talk with that person and pray with that person. Not as an outsider, not as a healthy person, whom they might have resented, but as one of them. Inviting them, as soon as they felt better, to come to her room and have coffee or tea and they would read together. So she found her spiritual strength, to endure pain and suffering, in her continuous service and care of others.

A high school freshman from Louisville, Kentucky once wrote John Walker because he was "very interested in becoming a bishop." The young man was a star acolyte in his parish, whose acolyte master had been trained at Washington National Cathedral. So it was only natural that the aspiring cleric write Bishop Walker, asking one of the country's most important religious leaders how he became Bishop of Washington and Dean of the National Cathedral. His moving reply dignifies the request with its self-revelation.

So You Want to Be a Bishop?

Dear Brian:

I read with interest your letter on how I became a bishop. Your question seems to be an easy one to answer but in fact it isn't. I have thought about it for several days, and I decided that I should begin at the beginning. When I was a little boy, my grandmother hoped that I might become a minister. Her father was a minister in the A.M.E. Church as were several of her brothers. Later when my family moved to Detroit our minister expressed the same hope. Thus was the idea planted in my mind.

I grew up in Detroit with a strong desire to become either a teacher or a psychiatrist. When World War II came and my two brothers went into the Army I began going to church again after several years absence. During those years I began to sense a very strong call from God to serve him as a minister. I accepted that call and began preparing for such a life.

I attended university for four years. During that time I became an Episcopalian and sought the Bishop's permission to begin formal studies for ordination. After graduating from college I studied at the Episcopal Seminary in Alexandria, Virginia for three years. After graduating I was ordained a deacon. Six months later I was ordained to the priesthood and became the rector of St. Mary's Church in Detroit, Michigan where I served for several years. In 1957 I moved to New Hampshire to serve the church there and to become a teacher in a church school called St. Paul's School. I remained there for 10 years and served the church in New Hampshire and Central America during the summer months. Also during that time I went with my wife and one-year-old son to live and work for a year in Uganda in East Africa. There I taught in a theological seminary. When we returned to the U.S. we moved here to the Washington Cathedral where I served as an Assistant to the Dean of the Cathedral, in charge of community and inter-religious work.

I had never thought about becoming a bishop. I am sure that I never wanted to be a bishop. It is easier to be a priest and work with one congregation. A bishop has to take care of all of the parishes, deacons, and priests in his diocese. He is responsible for the Cathedral, fund raising, diocesan programs, and work with other religious groups such as Roman Catholics, Lutherans, and others. He has to see to the development of youth work, Christian education, parish development, programs for the aging, the homeless, and he has responsibility for the spiritual tone of the diocese. And that is not all. He must see that a sufficient number of people are being trained as deacons and priests. He must ordain all the deacons and priest, confirm hundreds of people every year. I celebrate the Holy Eucharist at least one hundred times a year. I have weddings, baptisms, funerals, and meetings beyond imagining. If that were not enough, a bishop must do work for and with the National Church and the Church world-wide.

I have not written all of this to scare you away, I just want you to know why I wasn't seeking to be a bishop. It is a tremendously difficult and complex job. There are many people making demands on the time and energy of the person who holds this office.

I worked for five years as a Canon of Washington Cathedral. In May 1971, I was nominated by a committee of clergy and laypersons for the office of Suffragan Bishop (an assistant bishop without the right of succession to the office of Bishop of the diocese). On May 30th of that same year I was elected at a special convention of the diocese and on June 29, 1971 I was consecrated a bishop in the Church.

Naturally, I was nervous and frightened as to what the future would be like. I was very happy as a Suffragan Bishop since most of the problems were handled by the Diocesan Bishop who was my boss. I served for five years as Suffragan Bishop. That was a time of learning and training. I developed an understanding of the office and learned about the total work of the Church.

In 1976 I was elected Bishop Coadjutor (an assistant bishop with the right to become the Bishop of the diocese). A year later (July 1977) my boss, the Bishop, retired and I became the Sixth Bishop of Washington. On September 29th that year I was installed in the Bishop's Seat in Washington Cathedral.

Over the years God has been good to me as a servant in the church. I believe that at each stage our Lord through the Holy Spirit has called me to various positions in his Church. He calls every baptized Christian to service. It may be that he will call you to be a priest or even a bishop. Wait on His call and pray that you may hear it in the right way. Do not be afraid to listen. In the meantime be obedient to your parents and faithful to the Church and our Lord. And we will also pray for you here in this Cathedral that God will guide and protect you always.

Affectionately,
John T. Walker
Bishop of Washington

Chapter 5

The Beginning of Knowledge

*Then shalt thou understand…every good path when wisdom
entereth into thine heart, and knowledge is pleasant unto thy
soul.*—Proverbs 2:9-10

John Walker's parents, like so many of their generation, believed in the saving power of education. Young
John Walker started on the path toward salvation even
before he went to school. He already knew how to read
before 1st grade began. He was confident in his knowledge, and justifiably proud. Then he met Miss Lewis,
who taught him that it was dangerous to be smart
and black.

On the first day of school, six-year-old John Walker
was already breaking the rules. Miss Lewis had instructed
the class to look at the words, listen to her read, and
repeat what she said. John beat her to the punch, reading
to the teacher before she could read to him. No doubt he
expected Miss Lewis to appreciate his cleverness and
praise his initiative. Instead, she angrily upbraided him
for not following her instructions and then sent a note
home to his mother calling him "incorrigible." After
months of enduring the young teacher's scorn and wrath,
John ended up locked in a closet, forgotten for an
afternoon. When he failed to come home, his mother came
to school and let him out herself.

Walker knew first hand that education could be tyrannical. He grew up in a world in which it was generally understood that white children were more capable than black children. In his elementary school, the drama teacher cast black children in the roles of clown and cuckoo bird. When Noah's Ark was on stage, the parts of monkey and baboon were reserved for the likes of John Walker. Early on he understood the failure of mainstream American education to serve the entire republic. It was enough, he said in one address, to make you want to "take to the hills," to disengage from the whole affair and disappear into the safety of a world not shaped by the institutions of prejudice.

But it was not in John Walker's nature to run away from seemingly intractable situations. Instead, he always decided to stay and get on with the job. In the area of education, his early life experiences informed and inspired a life-long ministry of teaching and of administering teaching institutions. He knew from the start what he was up against. He also knew there was a better way.

He learned the way from Anna Lappeus, whose name destined her to teach high school Latin. When he described it in a speech to the National Association of Principals of Schools for Girls in the late 1960s, his Latin classroom was archetypal. The setting is an unpolluted city, with cherry blossoms lingering in the air. Children play under a clear blue sky. A Latin quiz is about to begin, but the teacher has only comforting words to say, relaxing her anxious pupils into remembering. Walker remembered her as a "gentle, warm, and wonderful" woman who cared about each of the students privileged enough to sit at her feet. He believed her when she promised that Latin trained the mind and preserved democracy, that knowledge for its own sake enlightened the mind and opened up new worlds. He went on to become a teacher like her.

After only a few brief years of parochial ministry in his native Detroit, Walker became a teacher of American history at St. Paul's School in Concord, New Hampshire. He was the first black member of "Millville," as the school community was known. For almost a decade Walker taught high school boys on the soccer field and in the dormitory—as well as the classroom. As a boarding school master (teacher), he was a natural. Adolescent boys opened their hearts to him; faculty and administrators relied on his wise counsel; staff members and family members came to expect him quietly to appear, ready to help, whenever trouble reared its head.

For two years Walker was the only black person at St. Paul's, a presence to be reckoned with. When people recalled his work there twenty years after he left, their memories were of his warmth, his humor, his even temper, his hospitality, his humanity. When both adults and adolescents encountered him, they were changed. To the afflicted, he brought comfort. To those who were too comfortable in their prejudice, he brought honesty and directness. He spoke the truth, in love. He had fun, too, and helped others find fun in their work and their play. Two years after he began teaching, St. Paul's first black students arrived. They found the way already paved and the support system they would need provided by John Walker.

Walker's classes in American history could be unorthodox. His lecture notes from his first semester at St. Paul's still exist, and they begin ordinarily enough. In faultless penmanship he detailed the points that had to be made...for about two months. Then there are talking points, then topics, until by midterm, there is nothing recorded at all. Was it growing confidence that led to this diminution? Or are his dwindling notes the sign of a first year teacher's exhaustion in the face of preparing a never-ending sequence of lesson plans? Both explanations may contain seeds of truth.

One of Walker's contemporaries, who went on to head the history department at St. Paul's wrote, "I often wondered just where he was going with his class. It was sometimes difficult to tell what the assignment was in American history as the class discussion wandered about." But on reflection, it was clear that Walker was teaching compassion as much as history. His method "related the content to the persons in the class." He "created a safe atmosphere in which to grow and have ideas." Walker himself said it best: "Let us get the order straight"—love your students, know your subject, teach with energy and conviction, impart the truth.

John Walker was a gentle but persistent catalyst for change in every educational institution or enterprise with which he came in contact. Even in the face of overwhelming evidence to the contrary, he believed that education was central to liberty and life. In an address to the Class of 1980 from his high school alma mater, Walker called education "a way back" for some and "a way of survival" for all. He called for the graduates of an inner city school not to "fall victim to bitterness." He challenged them not only to survive but to overcome, to work for justice, to live in the world of possibility. It must have been a poignant moment for him, standing at that graduation, his life an outward, visible sign of victory over an inward struggle with resentment and cynicism. Thirty-six years before, flaming cars and unruly mobs of angry young black men had cancelled his own graduation ceremonies at Cass Tech. He knew whereof he spoke. He taught everyone who would listen with the authentic authority of hard-won personal experience that had been mastered by the Spirit.

For Walker, education lay at the heart of not only the nation's well being but also the Church's mission. Like many others, he found education to be particularly important for the Anglican tradition. He noted that, historically speaking, Anglicanism had expected an educated clergy and assumed an educated laity. Religion based on feeling alone has always been suspect in the English Church. For Anglicans, faith must be not only experienced but also comprehended. Walker knew that every generation had to be educated anew in the value structure and deep meaning of Christian belief. Otherwise, he argued, faith devolves into little more than idiosyncratic emotion and wishful thinking.

Long after Walker left the classroom, he remained passionately involved with the process of education at the governance level. Serving on the boards of schools of every description, and being involved with the administration (not to mention the students) of the three Cathedral schools, Bishop Walker exercised an enormous influence over the education of thousands of children and adults. His ministry extended through decades of enormous upheaval in American educational philosophy and practice. He lived through and guided others in the transition from the narrow educational system of the 1950s to the integrated, co-educational, practical curricular, student-centered, multicultural schools of the twenty-first century.

Much of Walker's work was done in the somewhat rarified atmosphere of private schools, and in the even narrower niche of Church and Church-related schools. His support for these often elite institutions sometimes brought him into conflict with those who were ardent supporters of strictly public education. The delicate balancing act he regularly performed between public and private schools at least twice landed him in the pages of the *Washington Post.* As President of the National Coalition for Public Education and Religious Liberty (PEARL), Walker was installed as a legitimizing voice for an alliance of organizations opposed to government financial aid (including tuition tax credits) to private schools. (He had given the keynote address at the March 1973 conference that laid the blueprint for the organization's formation the following January.) Indeed, Walker had for many years been an outspoken opponent of direct government financial aid to private schools. In an interview, he suggested, however, that he might well be favorably disposed toward a plan that allowed taxpayers to deduct part or all of what they paid for private school tuition from their tax bills. His comments landed him in hot water with board members of PEARL who had a less nuanced view.

A few years later, Walker was moved to write the *Post's* editor in defense of the Black Student Fund, a charitable foundation he had chaired whose purpose was to fund scholarships for minority students to attend upper echelon private schools. Richard Cohen, a columnist for the paper, had written a fairly scathing critique of Mayor Marion Barry for chairing a Black Student Fund fundraising dinner at the same time he was overseeing a $75 million cut in the public school budget. Cohen argued that Barry's chairmanship implied that the best chance black kids in Washington had for getting a good education was to abandon the public school system and attend a private school instead.

The Bishop wrote,

> I am committed absolutely to public schools as the chief instrument of education in a democratic society. At the same time, I believe that Americans have a right to provide other kinds of education for their children. I believe that children from a pluralistic society such as ours should be able to mingle together in schools. This is most likely to happen right now in the independent and church schools. [Black people have a right] to seek alternative ways and places to educate their children… [I]t would be irresponsible (to say the least) for black people to lose a generation of their potentially brightest students by holding exclusively to the high commitment to public education, which I share.

He went on to argue that abolishing private schools and the Black Student Fund would do nothing in and of itself to improve the plight of public schools in Washington, D.C.

These teapot tempests are worth noticing only because they cast light on the way John Walker engaged the world. Without being eternally indecisive or frustratingly unpredictable in what he believed, he worked toward "both-and" solutions in a world increasingly given to "either-or" decisions. His approach was open to criticism by those who preferred to see issues in simpler terms. He irritated the doctrinaire, especially when continued reflection on his own experience and the counsel he received from others led him to change his mind. Rare indeed is a man who can be highly-principled and flexible. A man who knows when to compromise and when to hold his ground is the rarest of all.

In the final analysis, Walker's approach refuses to be drawn exclusively to either pole of the great debate among

African American leaders between conciliation and challenge. He wanted to work from within the system, building small coalitions of inclusive life, like Booker T. Washington. You might draw other parallels between Walker and Washington: both gained and used the respect of the (white) establishment to serve their race; both utilized extensively the wealth of (white) northern industrialists to aid their cause. But Walker's most important work was directed toward encouraging the oppressed to not accommodate themselves to the oppressor. Led by the convictions of his profound Christian faith, Walker called for the overthrow of oppression.

With what looks like, in retrospect, a stroke of genius, Walker combined the conciliatory methods of Booker T. Washington with the radicalism of that other great architect of black advancement, W. E. B. DuBois. Walker would certainly have sided with DuBois when the founder of the NAACP chided Booker T. Washington's accommodationist views. Walker did not work (at least out front) for Washington's emphasis on vocational education, nor did he care to wait patiently for the gradual emergence of black economic and political power in the coming social order.

Instead, Bishop Walker's words and deeds echo DuBois' concern for "the higher training and ambition of our [race's] brighter minds." DuBois worked to place African-American students on as level a playing ground as possible with their white peers. Like him, Walker devoted considerable time and energy to positioning black youth for lives of service within the country's leadership class, where he knew from his own experience that they could make a real difference in the lives of others. As Chairman, and later as board member for Washington's

Black Student Fund, Walker was instrumental in raising the institutional grants necessary to sustain a scholarship program that, during his years of leadership, supported over one hundred students in almost 50 schools to the tune of nearly a half million dollars in financial aid. Walker worked unceasingly to increase the diversity of the private school community he knew so well. In independent school settings, Walker argued, there was the best chance available for the creation of genuine communities of equality. He was instrumental in seeing that the equality being created was both racial and economic, and that access was only an interim step toward significant institutional change. Within the subset of independent religious schools, Walker believed, students of all races and creeds stood their best chance of being successfully inducted into the symbolic universes of Christian faith and democratic government.

Following his death, Walker's vision for education appeared alongside his most reflective portrait in the alumni magazine of the National Cathedral School. The editor outdid herself in the selection.

> The values that we uphold, and into which system we seek to induct our young, recognize the weakness and vulnerability of all people and especially of the young… Because we recognize these facts about humanity, we accept that we must structure our community life in such a way that the tendency toward self-aggrandizement and aggressive behavior are checked and these tendencies are balanced by the Christian ideals of love, trust, and forgiveness. This is the context within which our teaching and learning are set and in which our community exists.
>
> We are preparing our children for life in a complex, pluralistic society—one in which they

are asked to live with diversity in a nation with checks and balances; a nation of Christian and non-Christian; liberal and conservative; rights and counter-rights; justice and injustice; and, face it, good and evil. Is it not better to have them prepared to deal with all the complexities of such a nation and such a world? Is it not better to have them accept that they are not by nature better than others; that race, ethnic background, money, class, social position, intellect, nor any other artificiality give them special rights or greater justice?

My friends, I am convinced that we...can begin here a process of openness to new ideas, to bring about change in society. We can offer as the chief option for life—inclusiveness as opposed to exclusiveness; trust as opposed to distrust; love of each other; we can help them to make caring responses to each other; we can help to raise them up when they fall and set them on a course that may make this a better world for them and for their posterity.

In the place of argument, John Walker presented the same sentiment as a prayer in a dedication ceremony at Beauvoir School in 1973. In the midst of a severe energy crisis, Bishop Walker called administrators, students, parents, faculty, and alumni to see overwhelming power and cosmic significance of education. He prayed,

Almighty God, Who has given us the earth for our heritage and has endowed us with intelligence and physical strength, and also the hope and aspiration to turn energy into a good life: Grant us also the patience and the wisdom and the courage of our forbearers to use our strength and knowledge to move this people into a new place in the human sphere.

Bless these men and women who seek to achieve the goal of a healthy, peaceful, and happy humanity, that by the creative use of energy, they and we may assist in creating a new earth, so that our children and our grandchildren (and the many generations that follow) may benefit from the efforts of those who work for the advancement of the human Spirit.

Beyond that, help us all to achieve victory over greed, over oppression, and over war; and over that unfettered selfishness that leads us toward destruction.

Finally, help us—like you helped the prophets who lived of old, like you showed us in the Christ we serve today, like you gave strength to those who die for the sake of freedom in every age. So assist us with your grace that we make no peace with oppression, disease, or poverty as we work together to achieve a more abundant life. Amen.

In this 1973 address to the California Association of Indepen-
dent Schools, John Walker reflects on the changing values of
American education as the radicalism of the 1960s was being
digested by the nation's educational institutions. He displays
keen insight into the relationship between broader social
concerns and their effect on the way administrators organize
the educational process. As always, Bishop Walker eyes the past
with critical appreciation, assessing both its positive and
negative consequences for the present. The issues raised in this
speech remain at the forefront of discussion and controversy in
schools and society more than a quarter-century later.

To say that educational values are changing is to state not
only that which is obvious but to understand the case
itself. I suspect by now that we are all aware that educational concerns are much more than hard, provable,
statistical data. It is at the core about people, and values
and feeling. We know that the last 16 years have seen the
most extraordinary changes at all levels in the history of
human life. In 1957, Russia launched Sputnik I and sent
American educators scurrying to the drawing boards to
produce new curricula with a heavy stress on science,
math, and physics. It was believed that satellite was a
symbol of a deep failure in American education, with its
old-fashioned stress on those things designed to help
students to develop as people rather than to develop as
new technologists.

I recall one school where Greek, Latin, Religion,
History, and English always occupied a significant part
of the curriculum. In the decade following 1957, "hard
science" forced large scale cut-backs in the Classics, in
Religion, and in History. English remained intact, but
primarily because of usefulness in developing other and
important skills. Of course, many schools had been

prepared to sacrifice the humanities before 1957—in fact, many had already done so. But the universal stress on education for the sake of technological achievement had profound effects on education and values that are only now being felt.

Another significant change in values (in a general sense) seems to indicate a decided change in our time from what used to be an emphasis on the "helping professions" to money-making ones. I am completely aware that the early 1960s saw a rush into such activities as the Peace Corps, and the student turmoil of that period seemed to be predicated on a revolution against the depersonalization of the processes of education. But I suspect that, while these were genuine, they were at the same time residual elements from the post-war years when we were still stressing personal development and concern for others. Perhaps this was, in part, a result of President Roosevelt's last speech in which he talked about "developing the science of human relations as a way of developing the spirit of cooperation among people."

Recently I was involved in a discussion with a professor of psychology at American University who is engaged in analyzing student change. It is his contention that Law and Medicine are the most popular professional pursuits of a non-technical nature at that University. The questions that he has been asking seem to indicate that the reasons have to do with the apparent ease with which doctors and lawyers are able to make money while at the same time realizing significant comfort. I am not at all sure that this is a calculated act, but I suspect that the recent thrust of society has been more and more in money-making directions, rather than life-fulfilling ones.

If this is an accurate reading of what is happening at American University, and if it can in any sense be generalized, then it reflects a matter of deep concern. It means, in effect, that the concern our young people have had for changing society is disappearing. They seem less inclined to spend their lives looking for ways to make "the system" more responsive to human need. They seem to be becoming less concerned with making thought and action coincide. I see this having vital implications for the future.

A third area of concern (which is not unrelated to the other two) has to do with what we called in the '60s situation ethics. The purpose of those who promulgated that ethical concept was to free the individual from the guilt attached to a variety of actions which may not be ethical concerns themselves. The logic, however, of situation ethics suggested that no ethical position, no system of values could be transferred from one person or setting to another. So, for example, what our parents learned may have been right for them, but it could be disastrous for us. Ethicists like Joseph Fletcher suggested that our mores and folkways derive from a post-Victorian concept of ethics rather than from an open and honest society in which people are free to be themselves. Thus "doing one's own thing" becomes a matter of individual, rather than family or community concern.

Our young seem—by and large—to accept the concept with ease as being the way that most people behave anyway. I suspect they are right. We tend to select out of our common life and culture what we most remember positively, and whether someone else has deemed it to be so, is not all that important to us.

There was a time when we held a stock of common values such as *patriotism* (a genuine love for our nation and its high principles, or if that proves too difficult, at least a blind allegiance to the flag); *sexism* (a belief that "boys will be boys," which meant they would lie a little and of course, "sow their wild oats," while girls would be prim, proper, studious, and sexless); *homosexualism* (We knew it was there but kept it hidden or punished it severely); *racism* (Love your neighbor as yourself, but if you can't include blacks and other minorities then quote scripture loud and long); *progressivism* (It is good to go to school and learn as much as you can; this is virtuous.)

These values, good and bad, were developed at home, were nurtured in school, and given divine underpinnings in Church. Now all of these are suspect, and the life we knew is different, and the education that we seek for our children may reflect what we think more than what they need. This calls for careful thought.

In this sermon from Pentecost 1980, Bishop Walker develops a recurring theme of his ministry: the power of the Holy Spirit to overcome the barriers that separate the people of God from each other and from the divine. Late in the sermon, he reflects on his experience as an educator of young children. He finds their inability to live in community with each other to signify the depth and breadth of separation in human relationships, and he suggests that their failure to communicate was learned at the feet of their teachers.

It has been said throughout history that mankind is composed of solitary beings, that every person is born alone and dies alone. That is to say, the experience of the act of birth or the act of death is one in which each person has a unique experience, and in that sense cannot be shared. At the time of dying, the image of the crossing of a river or going through a valley is one in which each person must cross the river for him or herself. Each must go into and through the valley alone. No one can have that experience for you. It is uniquely one's own. Thus in the act of birth, wherein we become individuals, we must also remember that in a deeply personal way we become isolated. I am my own person.

From the beginning of man's effort to tell his story or to record his history we have witnessed a universal attempt to overcome this isolation. We have witnessed human beings seeking *a calling* somehow or other to find a measure of unity within the life that we all share together. That calling must be extraordinarily strong, for everything that we are and everything that we do seems to set us apart from one another.

We seem trapped in our very bodies. We must protect them from danger, and the dangers that we see lurking about us are not simply wild animals or natural elements—they are other human beings. Very early in the life of a person he comes to see other humans, animals, or nature as forces inimical to his own health, safety, and welfare. This is thought to be ameliorated within the family community where one trusts mother and father and immediate siblings, and that extends itself to include grandparents and even cousins and uncles and aunts and members of a tribe.

But always and wherever we are seeking somehow or other to overcome those elements that divide us, that keep us apart, that set us in isolation. Thus we seek unity within family, we seek unity within tribe or within a larger community, and ultimately within nations. But even there we recognize that we think our own thoughts. We understand language in our own ways. We recognize disagreement and we seek to overcome it.

Every human experience is potentially an isolating event. Even religion itself has been seen historically as that which divides rather than that which unites. And some would say that the rise of the modern nation-state in the west was one of the worst things that happened to us in terms of our search for unity, because it has divided us along national and ethnic lines, whereas, earlier on, we had been able to identify ourselves with the much larger idea of empire. There was the Holy Roman Empire, and before that the Roman Empire itself—both expansive entities with which a variety of peoples could identify, both providing an identity within which we could group ourselves, both providing a haven, as it were, for us lonely, isolated persons.

The Hebrew-Christian story, as is true of many others in the world, is an effort to overcome the separation, too. Our faith is the story of how people can be united in God, and through God, and to God—and thus to each other. But having said so, one recognizes immediately that there is a certain arrogance in that statement, for we are not reconciling ourselves to God. God was in the world, in the Creation, in the leading of the Hebrew people across the Red Sea into the promised land, in the kings, in the prophets; and God was in Christ uniting and reconciling the world unto himself.

It is in this light that the Pentecost story and the Pentecost event must be understood, and against that background we would also paint one other picture: the picture of our Lord in the last days of his life and his time on earth speaking with his disciples. In the last days before his Crucifixion, he talked with them about who he is and about the task that is before them. Then, when he appears to them after the Resurrection, he speaks to them with these morals. He speaks to them in the form of a prayer to the Father, when he says, "Father, I pray for these and not only these but I pray especially for these that they might be in me as I am in you and that they might be one so that the world might believe that you have sent me."

This Christ figure, when the last hours of his time on earth are at hand, when he is about to leave his beloved disciples, when he is preparing to ascend to the Father, this Christ prays for unity, and Pentecost is the story of unity.

We have heard it said that there is nothing in the Scriptures that provides us with answers to specific problems and questions, and that may be true. But all of our searching on earth, all of our longing for unity, finds itself resident in one Christian story—the story of Pentecost. St. Luke writes in the Book of the Acts of the Apostles, "When the day of Pentecost had come they were together in one place and suddenly there came a sound from heaven like the rush of a mighty wind, and it filled all the house where they were sitting and there appeared to them tongues of fire resting on each of them and they were filled with the Holy Spirit and they began to speak in other tongues as the spirit gave them utterance."

And then we hear this: "Now there were dwelling in Jerusalem devout men from every nation under heaven," and further, "At this sound, the multitude came together, and they were confused because each one heard the wonderful works of God in his own tongue, in his own language, albeit they were from Mesopotamia and Egypt and Cyrene and from the outermost parts of the Roman Empire."

Now, were we to examine that passage of Scripture with some care, we might end up confused ourselves, because we would wonder if the passage really intends to say that each member of the multinational congregation gathered in Jerusalem on that first Pentecost could actually hear the Apostles' message in his own tongue (in Greek and in Hebrew and in Latin or whatever language they spoke). In that case, their confusion would have stemmed out of the fact that they knew that the Apostles were peasants from Galilee, simple men who would not have the education or experience necessary to speak in the languages of Athens and Rome.

On the other hand, the language of Acts seems to suggest that the people of that first Pentecost were instead caught up in an emotional religious experience, even going so far as to suggest that they were babbling nonsensically. But somehow, says St. Luke, out of the confusion of ecstatic sound flowing from the Spirit-filled Apostles, people of every nationality heard for themselves the wonderful works of God. In this way of looking at the Scripture, the Holy Spirit was working in Pentecost to give everyone new insight, a new understanding, and a new power. It was the power to end the forces that separated them from each other. The power of the Holy Spirit overcame the power of separation, and with separation gone, the people of Pentecost were able to understand in a new way what it was that God was calling them to do.

The confusion of Pentecost came not only out of the fact that people didn't understand how the Apostles had managed to learn Latin and Greek and all the other languages of the empire; the confusion came because they were uncertain. They were bewildered. They had known this Jesus. They had recently known him in the Resurrection. They had learned to call him the Christ, and now he was gone and yet he had left them a task—to go into all the world and preach the gospel and bring unity to God's people wherever they were. Their confusion stemmed from the fact that they had no clue about how they were supposed to get that job done.

How would you go about it? How do you overcome the barriers of language, ethnic background, culture, and religion and all the things that confront us in the world? How do you overcome those things so that somehow or other God's message becomes clear? In the bewilderment of Pentecost, they heard and they knew. For Jesus had said he would send the Spirit of Truth, the Comforter, to stay with them to guide them into all truth. And Jesus had promised that through the Spirit he would overcome all the barriers that confronted his disciples in the world.

It was on that note of hope that a small band of people could proceed from Jerusalem into all the world—so much so that 2,000 years later, we gather here in this place—and in places like it all over the earth—to celebrate the unity that God sent to us in his Holy Spirit on that day of Pentecost and ever continues to do so.

But what is the message in this for us, for you and for

me, in our own day? Lord knows we have enough confusion. We have so much confusion in our world that it makes that time 2,000 years ago pale by comparison. It would, I suppose, make Peter and John and James and all of the others tremble before the power of such confusion as we know. You well know that here, even in our own land where there is at least one official language, we are unable to understand and communicate with one another. How, then, are we to communicate with the Iranians or the Russians or the Chinese? We have difficulty communicating with those whom we call our allies. How then do we communicate with those whom we call the enemy? How then do we somehow or other through diplomacy (or whatever is available to us) begin to crawl under or climb over the barriers that separate us in our time?

Sometimes as I work with small children here on this Cathedral Close, and as I travel around the country meeting with students in other places, it makes me wonder. It is so difficult even for the very young (or maybe especially for the very young) to communicate across the barriers that separate them, many of which we have given them by our own teaching. It is so difficult for husbands and wives, for parents and children, to understand and communicate—how much more so can we expect nations, who speak different languages and have different cultural backgrounds and different religions, to overcome those things that separate them.

And yet the message of Pentecost—the message of the risen Christ—remains the same, for his prayer is and always will be that we may be one; that we may somehow or other learn how to live together in harmony and peace; that we may somehow or other share the goods of the world, so that none would go to bed hungry; that somehow or other war may become unnecessary and truth may prevail on the earth; that there may be so much compassion and love among us that we can become what the Spirit calls us to be: witnesses to God's reconciling love for the world.

Now there are no specific answers here. The Scriptures don't tell us whether if we do it through education we will succeed. The Bible doesn't tell us whether we will succeed if we stop building arms. On such matters, the Word of God is silent. We only know this: that we are called upon to live in harmony and peace and love with one another. And we know that such a life means at the very least that we must subdue the self, that we must put pride aside, that we must stop thinking first of our own welfare, that we must put greed out of our experience. Even politicians realize that nothing is accomplished without sacrifice. It takes money and power to solve the world's economic and military troubles. It takes the effort of many people working together if there is to be any real accomplishment.

We cannot do it alone, but we must begin somewhere. The sacrifice must begin with those who have something to sacrifice. Fasting must be done by those who are not already starving to death. The hard work of waging peace must be done by those who are strong enough to put aside their pride. We must now allow those elements of hate that have been so long with us to dominate our lives, preventing us from knowing the unity of life in the One True God. On this day of Pentecost, let us pray together that we might hear of God's mighty work, each in our own tongue. Let us pray that the Spirit might cut through all of the barriers that separate us, barriers of language, of religion, of base culture, of politics, of law, and of hate so that we might know peace and unity in our time. Amen.

*In this brief but touching homily, John Walker recalls his days
as a Master at St. Paul's School in New Hampshire. The occasion is Children's Day at the Washington National Cathedral,
a community celebration of the Body of Christ's youngest members. Bishop Walker captures the spirit of the day by opening a
window on his own understanding and enjoyment of the rest-
less, raucous lives of children. Celebrating the gift of children,
he points out to the grownups in attendance, means taking care
of children everywhere.*

All of us, whatever our religious views, hold one concept
in common with regard to children. From the God we
serve, we derive a belief that children need to be loved,
need to be cared for, need to be educated. I am reminded
of a scene in Mexico City. When you drive out of the city
toward the north, you come to a series of signs along the
way. Each sign begins with the phrase: "To love a child
is…" Then the idea is finished off in a way that would
make all of us feel perfectly at home and with which all of
us agree. To love a child is to feed her or him. To love a
child is to celebrate the child's birthday. To love a child is
to educate him or her. To love a child is to be concerned
about that child's health. To love a child is to see that the
child has a bed to sleep in. To love a child is to teach the
child to read or to sing or to dance or to recite poetry. We
say all of these all the time, in this country and around
the world.

And yet it remains a fact of life that around the world
more children go to bed hungry every night than otherwise. Sometimes we say these things rather glibly, but the
real facts remain: around the world too many children are
sick, and without medical care; around the world too many
children are homeless, without parents, without that
continuity of love that makes growing up possible, that
makes life for the young very special. But we need not go

very far around the world to find these ugly facts about life. We can find them in the city of Washington, where too many children die at the very beginning of their lives; where too many children are without good health care, good food; where too many children lack an education, a decent place to sleep.

So there is a challenge for all of us adults here who claim to worship a God who loves and cares, a God who calls upon *us* to love and to care. There's a challenge for us to work together, to see whether or not—in this city— that every child might go to bed well fed, that little children might have necessary inoculations against disease, that little children might have a good education, that those children who do not have parents might find adoptive parents to offer them the love and care that we believe is necessary to life and growth and development.

So I call upon all of the adults here today to give and to work and to struggle; to talk to congressmen and senators; to talk to the mayor and the councilmen; to talk in churches, in synagogues, and mosques; to talk so that all of us together might make an impact upon this city. Perhaps we might be able to develop here a model for the country, a model that demonstrates the deepness of our love and our care for these little ones who have been given into our hands and into our love.

And now the children. Children's Day is a celebration, and I hope you are going to remember that. Children's Day is not a time when we want to be altogether serious (even if we have to be a little bit; forgive us for that for a moment). It is a time to say happy birthday; it is a time to say prayers of thanks to God for who you are and to thank you just for being our children because of the joy that you bring into our hearts. It's a holiday and everybody knows what a holiday is.

Well, if you don't let me explain. Many years ago (when I was much younger than I am now), I was a teacher in a school in far-off cold New England in the northeastern part of the United States. It's a very cold place. The winters were very long. Darkness covered us 14 hours a day.

Although the fall was very beautiful, we had a number of days that were holidays. In fact one of the most beautiful holidays of all came around Thanksgiving time. It was called "Black Ice Holiday." On that day at 9 in the morning an 18-year-old boy would go out on the ice on his ice skates, and he (with a teacher) would measure the ice to see whether it could hold 800 people. And when he skated back in and said yes, immediately after the service and chapel everybody went on the ice. Five-hundred and fifty children and 250 adults! There were mothers with babies, and those who couldn't skate had chairs and they would push the chairs across the ice so that they would not fall—all of us were on the ice, and it was a great and glorious sight, and it was a holiday.

Now in January, winter was well upon us and there was no holiday that was regularly scheduled. So we began to pray that the head of the school would take pity on us and give us a holiday. In fact many of the children (the older boys) would not do their homework because they were betting on a holiday. The holiday was usually announced in this way. The custom reflects again the ancient and long love that Christian and Jewish people and Muslim people have had for children. If I were the minister of the day, the headmaster of the school (the principal) would call me, and he would say, "John, will you read *the prayer* this morning?"

And then 550 boys (in those days it was all boys, now it would be boys and girls) would come into chapel looking very dejected and they would kneel and they would say prayers. You could almost hear them thinking, "Maybe today will be the holiday." And sure enough it would be.

Now this is the way they found out. I would say lots of prayers, and we would sing a hymn, and then finally I would say, "Almighty God, who has promised that the city of Jerusalem shall be filled with the laughter of children playing in the streets thereof..." and you would never get to "the streets thereof," because every boy in that room understood right away that a holiday had been proclaimed! A great shout would go up all over that chapel, and they would run out and have that day, their day, to do whatever they liked.

Children's Day is like that. It's a holiday. It's a day of balloons and it's a day of singing and dancing and joy, for we are terribly grateful to God for having given you to us. I pray, and we all pray together, that we will never forget what it means to love a child. To love a child means to celebrate that child in all the ways that love knows how. Thank you for being here.

2

3

4

6

7

9

10

12

13

14

15

16

17

19

20

22

23

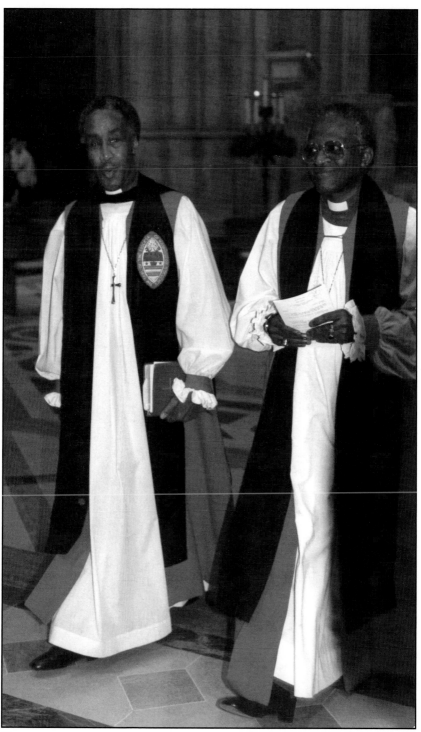

Photo Captions

1. Bishop John Walker writing in his cathedral office.

2. Bishop Walker's parents: Mattie and Joseph Walker, 1963.

3. With seminary classmates, Virginia Theological Seminary, 1952.

4. Track Coach John Walker with a record-setting sprinter at St. Paul's, May 1958.

5. The Rector of St. Mary's Church, Detroit, visits parishioners.

6. With 1 $1/2$-year-old son Tommy, in Uganda. On sabbatical from St Paul's, Walker taught for a year at Bishop Tucker Theological School, in Mokona.

7. Maria and then Canon Walker with their children Carli (left), Ana Maria (center), and Tommy (right) in their Washington, D.C. home.

8. Happy Wedding Day for Maria and John Walker, June 23, 1962, in St. Paul's Cathedral, Detroit.

9. The Bishop of Washington preaching from the Canterbury pulpit.

10. (Inset) The newly Consecrated Bishop Suffragan of Washington, John Walker, celebrates the Eucharist, 1971.

11. The Bishop kneels in prayer at the Altar in the Cathedral at his Installation as the Diocesan, 1977.

12. Ever the teacher and Good Shepherd, Bishop Walker loved engaging children and young people in dialogue about their faith and religion.

13. Speaking during the liturgy for the children's chapel service of Beauvoir School in the Great Crossing of the Cathedral.

14. Special Christmas homily for young people.

15. Taking questions from young people in the Cathedral's St. Joseph's Chapel.

16. The great preacher and Civil Rights leader, the Rev. Dr. Martin Luther King, Jr., with then Canon Walker, and diocesan communications director Jack Chapin (right). Dr. King preached in the cathedral on March 31, 1968. This photo was taken just four days before Dr. King's assassination in Memphis, Tenn.

17. Participants march for an end to apartheid in South Africa in Washington, D.C. (L-R) Randal Robinson, Bishop Walker, Roger Wilkins, Judith Claytor.

18. Following the liturgy celebrating the Bicentennial of the United States in 1976, Bishop Creighton accompanies Queen Elizabeth II and President Gerald R. Ford out of the Cathedral, followed by Bishop Suffragan Walker accompanying Prince Philip and First Lady Betty Ford.

19. Archbishop of Canterbury Robert Runcie with Bishop Walker, 1980.

20. Archbishop Desmond Tutu and Bishop Walker greet former Presiding Bishop Edmond L. Browning.

21. Bishop Walker with President Jimmy Carter, 1978.

22. President Anwar al-Sadat of Egypt (right) greets Bishop Walker in Cairo on his visit there in November 1979.

23. Anglican consultation. (L-R) The Rt. Rev. Peter James Lee, Bishop of Virginia; Bishop Walker; and The Rt. Rev. Samir Kafity, Bishop of Jerusalem & the Middle East, 1988.

24. Bishop Walker and Archbishop Desmond Tutu in procession in the National Cathedral, during Advent in the 1980s.

25. Bishop Walker in August 1989.

Chapter 6

Blessed Are the Poor

He hath filled the hungry with good things.—Luke 1:53

It was cold and wet in Washington in the spring of 1968. For a solid month it rained on the three thousand or so people living in Resurrection City. They were there without Martin, without Bobby, squatting on federal land within sight of President Johnson, who was in a quagmire of his own. They had the right permits to occupy West Potomac Park. It was all quite organized and legal. They had a post office and a first-aid station; a town hall and a cultural center. They all had a roof over their head. That was about all they had.

They had come to show the nation what is was like to be poor—poor in Appalachia, poor in inner-city Detroit, poor on southwestern Indian reservations. They meant to push legislation into being that would move beyond civil rights to address the fundamental economic injustice that lay at the heart of the nation's discontent. What they got was muddy and discouraged. After six weeks, park police ran them out of town, and then a great dream all but died in the midst of the tear gas and riot gear that sent them packing.

John Walker, though, kept on dreaming. He watched it all unfold firsthand, Resurrection City and the events that led to its foundation. In the bitter cold of February he had worked in Southeast D.C. to calm tempers and stop police from charging angry young black men rioting in the street. From the cool stone of the National Cathedral's Canterbury Pulpit he preached about it, too, and in no uncertain terms. By May he was warning God-fearing, middle class Washington that the "expressive violence" plaguing the nation's cities was but a foretaste of the revolutionary violence to come as black Americans grew increasingly frustrated. He identified Resurrection City, that Eastertide 1968, as one last appeal to the nation's conscience, one last chance for mainstream America to understand the plight of the poor.

Resurrection City was the centerpiece of the Poor People's Campaign, announced by the Rev. Dr. Martin Luther King, Jr. five months before his assassination. The mass live-in on the banks of the Potomac was to have launched the next phase of the civil rights movement. It was to have been the first act of a coordinated, three-part effort to change the hearts of America's citizens, the structure of America's corporations, and the focus of the American dream. At a news conference announcing the campaign, Dr. King said,

> America is at a crossroads of history and it is critically important for us as a nation and a society to choose a new path and move upon it with resolution and courage. It is impossible to under-estimate the crisis we face in America. The stability of a civilization, the potential of free government, and the simple honor of men are at stake. Those who serve in the human rights movement, including our Southern Christian Leadership Conference, are keenly aware of the increasing bitterness and despair and frustration that threaten the worst chaos, hatred, and violence any nation has ever encountered. In a sense, we are already at war with

and among ourselves. Affluent Americans are locked in the suburbs of physical comfort and mental insecurity. Poor Americans are locked inside ghettos of material privation and spiritual debilitation. And all of us can almost feel the presence of a kind of social insanity which could lead to national ruin. The true responsibility for the existence of these deplorable conditions lies ultimately with the larger society and much of the immediate responsibility for removing the injustices can be laid directly at the door of the federal government.

The Rev. Canon John Walker was listening.

On Sunday, March 31, 1968, the eighty-two men of the captured *USS Pueblo* were in a North Korean prison compound. In Khe Sahn, U.S. Marines held their ground as General Westmoreland launched the heaviest air and artillery bombardments of the Vietnam War, driving three divisions of Ho Chi Minh's best troops back across the border, effectively ending the last engagement of the Tet Offensive. In the White House, President Johnson was getting ready to address the nation with the news that he would curtail fighting in South Vietnam, and that he would step down after one term in office. At the National Cathedral, Canon Walker was listening to a sermon by Martin Luther King, Jr.

Walker was listening to the idea that poverty was as much a matter of pride as of paychecks—a fact he knew well from personal experience as a sharecropper's son from Georgia. He listened well to Dr. King's growing insistence that the escalating war in Vietnam was a burden on the backs of those who were already weak from malnutrition, infant mortality, alienation, and hope abandoned. He was listening to Dr. King talk about the coming revolution from the very pulpit that would one day be his as Bishop of Washington and Dean of the Cathedral Church of St. Peter and St. Paul. He heard and understood that there was enough of everything to share and then some; enough of everything, that is, except compassion.

The address that morning, titled "Sleeping Through a Revolution," would be Dr. King's last Sunday sermon. In it he moved with sure steps from Africa, to the inner city, to the rural South, to stony New England—an uncanny recitation of John Walker's travels. His text was from Revelation ("Behold, I make all things new!"), but his most telling use of Scripture was in his analysis of a parable from Matthew. King looked at the story of Abraham and Dives, the Old Testament patriarch in Paradise talking with another rich man, this one being tormented in the fires of perdition because he had consistently ignored a poor beggar at his table. Nothing wrong with being rich, King said; something very wrong with not seeing that your brother is hungry.

Conscientious objectors in the war on poverty, King concluded, go straight to hell. John Walker heard that, too.

But more than the content of King's sermon resonated with John Walker. As he formed his identity and practiced his approach to ministry, he caught the spirit of Martin Luther King, Jr., who refused to give up on his country and on Christ's Church. In the course of his ministry, Walker carried on a quiet but never-ending campaign against poverty, using every tool at his disposal. He used his wallet and his home, his Chair as the Ecclesiastical authority of the Diocese of Washington, his visibility as Dean of the Cathedral, his television show, his involvement in the affairs of the National Church, his leadership positions in ecumenical organizations, his power of persuasion, his pulpit and lectern and study.

He structured the Diocese of Washington to serve as an agent for social change, not merely responding to crisis but anticipating the future and the human need that would be created by actions in the present. He called for the Church not to shy away from conflict, but to boldly take up the poor's cause. It was the right thing to do, he argued, because it is what Jesus did. Quoting the unorthodox German pastor and theologian Christoph Blumhardt, Walker told the diocesan convention in 1983, "Jesus set his hope on the poor."

Walker knew and taught that it was not enough to offer money from a distance and platitudes from on high. "If we want to follow Jesus," Walker told his people, "our hands must touch the hands of the poor. We must know the poor and not content ourselves with social theories and pious illusions. Know the poor and you begin to know Christ. Know the poor and you begin to know the darkness of our collective existence as a society. Know the poor and you begin to understand that the Church itself is poor before God, that…we still do not really recognize the Sovereign Lord who comes to us as the Crucified One."

On this point, Walker's theology is quite sophisticated. As he understood Christian faith, people come to believe in the risen Christ only as they encounter him in caring for the poor. He knew many folks like the women at the tomb, running away from God, afraid to believe lest they be disappointed one more time. As the chief evangelist of the diocese, he encountered people practically every day who were looking for a reason to believe, for a sign that it might be true. The sign, he told them, was the community of faith itself, "ministering to the sick, the homeless, the hungry, the unwashed, the unloved." The evidence they wanted—that all of us want—is revealed as we become the Body of Christ, the risen Lord in every time and place." Thus he established a dialectic of belief and action: as we come to believe, we serve; as we serve, we come to believe.

And so John Walker always preached about the poor. On Christmas and on Thanksgiving, at church conventions and Senate hearings, as great events unfolded for the nation and as seasons turned and families left their summer houses and looked back home toward another busy year. He preached most fervently about the poor, however, in Eastertide, the Great Fifty Days when the Church celebrates the presence of living Christ in its midst. For John Walker, the Church's words of ancient Easter greeting were good news to the poor.

"He is risen!" is no interesting anachronism of second century liturgy, he would say. They are not just happy words for well-dressed Episcopalians on their way to Easter Brunch. They are instead a revolutionary statement of God's love, and an assurance that God's love makes a difference in the world. Those with theological sophistication (and John Walker was one of them, a deeply scholarly man whose learning always informed but never overwhelmed his mission) will find here Orthodoxy and good, old-fashioned Social Gospel. But it is more than that.

John Walker's theology of resurrection is a remarkable statement of belief in a century dominated by insecurity and war; a hundred years of advancement in technology that led most people on the planet nowhere. Can his faith in God, and ultimately his faith in God's Church, be enough to launch a new millennium of faithful action on behalf of God's Chosen People, the poor? If you listen to his words, you begin to believe it just might be possible. You begin to believe that Resurrection City was not a failure after all, and that the Poor People's Campaign did not end in 1968 after all, but goes on.

Bishop Walker's 1979 Easter sermon ends like this:

When Jesus died on the cross and rose from the
dead he revealed the ultimate truth about God and
about humanity. He revealed our weaknesses, our
vulnerability to sin and death. He saw us in the
glare of our sin even as we demanded his death
and executed him. He also revealed God's love for
all of his children. He forgave us from the cross and
after he was raised up demonstrated further God's
love of us by securing for us a place in his eternal
kingdom. By his death and resurrection he assured
us that sin and death would no longer control our
lives. That is the good news encapsulated in those
three little words: He is Risen!

But perhaps even now you are not convinced.
Perhaps you will say that we are not as unsophisti-
cated as they were. We know more than they did.
We are not so insecure about life as they were.
Perhaps they were grasping at straws in the wind
or a plank in the sea. We who break the sound
barrier as we jet to Europe; we who can explore
outer space do not suffer from the same insecuri-
ties. Some have even concluded that we do not need
a Savior—indeed we do not, they say, need a God!
We are all that we need.

How true are these conclusions? For example,
how equipped are we to deal with our children
and suicide, with our children and sex, with our
children and drugs? Are we truly secure when we
must live behind walls, behind iron screens, barbed
wire enclosures and buy millions of handguns to
protect ourselves? How secure are we when we
must spend the wealth of nations on nuclear arms
in order to feel safe? Does our ability to destroy life
on earth give us security? No! We share in the
dilemma that Paul explains so well. If our salvation and deliverance are in our hands, solved by

our ability to either keep the law or to do good works then we are lost. It is by his grace and love expressed in the cross and resurrection that we receive salvation. Our security is in the hands of God. It is the Risen Christ who calls us to service in his name who also delivers us from "this body of death."

As his servants we are called to a ministry of sharing, of reconciliation and of love. As a result of our salvation we seek to do ministry in His name. Do we hear the cry of those in our own land who are hungry, homeless, dying of cancer and AIDS or at the hands of gunmen? Are they not hungry for Christ's message of hope? Would they not give anything to hear someone say "He is Risen!"—to say, "You are loved, wanted, cared for by God?"

Do we preach and live the gospel of our Lord so that his grace and love may be seen and believed? The world is hungry for food and for love. It is hungry for homes and the sheltering arms of one who cares. There is need for justice and freedom in the world. Whether one lives in South Africa, Afghanistan, the Soviet Union, Cuba (or almost anywhere in the world) is not the cry for deliverance? Was it not the faith in the risen Christ that sustained the oppressed and enslaved throughout history? Remember the peasants in pre-Soviet Russia, the working class in pre-19th century England, the slaves in America—you can multiply the examples for yourself! Karl Marx said religion was their opiate keeping them enslaved. Marx did not understand that without their faith, they would have died. He did not understand that justice was as important to them as food.

Their true hope is in the Risen Christ (as ours is), which we claim in our time to be the Body of Christ. Their hope then in some real sense is in us. We can help give reality to three little words: *He is*

Risen! We can, as ministers of our risen Lord, show that a true translation of those words is this: God loves us. He wills that we share in his ministry of reconciliation, that we share what he has given to us with his children who are in need, that we console one another in our grief, that we claim justice for all who live without it. He loves us. He is risen and He lives!

Insofar as we believe, then He can be revealed in us.

Like all prophets, John Walker was keenly aware of what people expected to hear from God on certain occasions. In this Thanksgiving sermon from 1986, he draws the congregation in with the comforting words about divine providence and provision that are appropriate to the holiday. And then, in a rhetorical move reminiscent of the Old Testament prophet Amos (albeit with reason rather than thunder), he snags his listeners on their own presuppositions: the things for which they think they have gathered to give thanks turn out to be the very things for which God cares not. Those who thought they were prosperous are revealed in their poverty of Spirit. And so Thanksgiving, that most traditional of holidays, becomes a vehicle for a radical proclamation of good news to the poor.

It gives me pleasure to welcome all of you here to this service of worship on Thanksgiving Day. This, as you know, is a very important day in our lives and nation. It is the day when people travel from all parts of the world to return to their families and friends to give thanks on this day of days for all the gifts that God has made available to us as a people.

That portion of St. Matthew's Gospel read this morning has these important lines in it, "Therefore do not be anxious saying, 'What shall we eat?' or 'What shall we drink?' or 'What shall we wear?' For the gentiles seek all these things; and your heavenly Father knows that you have need of them all. But seek first His kingdom and His righteousness, and all these things shall be yours as well."

These words of our Lord recorded in this sixth chapter of the Gospel according to St. Matthew are a call to faith. The words seem to call us away from careful planning, away from thinking about survival. And this is difficult for us, because we have grown up in our time (and I suspect it was true of those who lived in our Lord's time, as well), grown up in an atmosphere that says that you must think about tomorrow. You must plan for tomorrow. You must put away something for a rainy day.

And perhaps, even more especially in those times than today, one had to think about survival. There were forces that work out there in the world that were designed to cut your life short. There were disease, pestilence, and war. There were those who would simply do you in because the opportunity presented itself. So, survival was the name of the game. It was that which people worked for on a daily basis. While it may be so, that our Lord is calling us away from careful planning and away from survival, in fact there is something even more important that we need to keep in mind. For, in fact, what His words do is to call us into a relationship of trust in God and into an awareness of His Kingdom. We shall address this idea again in a moment, for it touches on the core of our being as Christians in America, but let us look first to the words of Jesus and to Him who is speaking.

To whom are they addressed? To us who have lived to the near end of the twentieth century? The Gentiles of His own time? (He mentions them in His words.) Or to His brothers and sisters in the Jewish community? I think that it is clear they are not addressed specifically to us or to the Gentiles of His time. All of Jesus' words seem to be addressed to those who were around Him. They may have applicability to our own times, but that has to do with the universality of the words, not because He was directing them to or at us. He is not addressing them to the Gentiles, either, for the Gentiles would not be prepared to hear them. So He must be addressing them to His Jewish contemporaries.

Always Jesus calls His followers back to their roots as a Jewish people, as members of God's holy chosen people. He has looked at His own generation and seen a growing dependence on things: on money, and worldly possessions for example. He recognizes that, even as they come from year to year to give thanks for their salvation at the Red Sea, there is ample evidence of worldliness in the exchange of money, the sale of appropriate creatures for sacrificial offerings. Hence, in both private and public life, there seems to be an increasing dependence on possessions, on money, and on things that money can buy. We are reminded that Isaiah warned his people also, for they became equally dependent upon foreign alliances for their military security. Isaiah calls them back to faith, to the belief that God is their King. To the people of Israel, Isaiah makes it clear that their security is found in God and God alone.

Jesus compares the behavior of his people in his age to that of the Gentiles, the non-believers who are concerned about survival first, about storing goods and money, who show little concern about any God (certainly not One who resembles the one true God). Thus, Jesus chides His friends, "Do not be like them. You worship the true God of Creation who, therefore, knows your needs before you ask—your need to eat, to drink, to be clothed, or to have shelter—for thus did He create you. Develop your relationship to Him. Understand His will for your life. Do not think first about survival; He created you, and He will give you the strength, the knowledge, and the tools for survival. Thinking first about survival can only lead to greed, to the accumulation of things and, ultimately, to the sin of pride in your accomplishments, or the sin of despair if you fail. Therefore, do not think first about self; think first about God and His Kingdom and all else will come."

In the Kingdom to which Jesus refers, everything will be as it should be. There will be no wars, no injustice, no poverty, no hunger, no lack of shelter. Instead, all creatures will be gathered in a loving relationship to God and to each other—all creatures giving thanks for God's love and mercy and for the sharing of His life. That kingdom is not come yet. But it has already begun to dawn. And in order for that Kingdom to be fully understood and fully realized, it must break into our own time and space. God's kingdom, inaugurated by the resurrected Lord, must continue to dawn here and now. We must cease our search for our own security, for our own survival; for our Lord said it well, "He who seeks his life will lose it; but he who loses his life for my sake will surely find it." We must cease in our efforts to claim for the few the resources created for all, we few who are strong enough to force others out of the market; powerful enough to force others to be our servants and our slaves; dominant enough to cause them suffering or even death. We must cease our wars of aggrandizement or aggression, for God's Kingdom is a Kingdom of peace, a Kingdom of sharing and love.

This is Jesus' message to His people two-thousand years ago. It is a message as old as history and as new as our own day. Hence, it is a message to us.

It is well for us to recall these words of our Lord as we gather from around the world to give thanks to God for His blessing. We do so here because this call to faith reminds us of what it is that we give thanks for. Today, some will say that we should be thankful for our nation, for its strong position militarily and economically in the world. Others will want to give thanks for liberty, for family and friends, for good fortune, for homes and for good food, for warm clothes and for pure drinking water.

While all of these are appropriate subjects for our gratitude, they come, do they not, under the heading of the very things Jesus asked us not to seek first. Military and economic strength are subject to far too many human conditions to put our faith in such things. Because the economy is likely to fluctuate from day to day, we may be strong one week and not so strong the next. Further, because of the military drain on our economic life—that is, because we spend an inordinate amount of our wealth on defense—we are unable to care for the millions of children and adults who are victims of unemployment and of greed. Thus, the gap widens between rich and poor, between haves and have-nots.

What, therefore, should the unemployed be thankful for? For what should the homeless and the hungry in our land give thanks? For our military strength as their children go hungry? For our free enterprise system as they freeze to death in the streets? My friends, it is unconscionable that a nation as rich as ours has so many people in it who face the winter without shelter and without regular food. There are more such than ever before in our history. There are more infants who will die from disease, lead poisoning, and lack of proper food than should be true of any nation as wealthy as ours.

Yes, we give thanks for our freedoms; all of our freedoms are tremendously important. Yes, we give thanks that we have the security, such as it is. Yes, we give thanks for a system that permits individual activity and freedom, providing us with a democratic life. But should we put all of our trust in nuclear weapons or any other kind? Should we hide the unemployed and the hungry and pretend that they do not exist? Should we put all of our trust and faith in any system created by human beings? Given the fact that we humans are flawed, any system that we are likely to create will itself be flawed. Should we not, rather, as a nation, restore those funds taken away by government so that our national demonstration of concern happens intentionally every day and not just during the Holy Seasons of the year or on Thanksgiving Day?

We are a responsive people. When a hunger or poverty crisis hits, we raise billions of dollars to feed the hungry, both at home and abroad. We travel great distances to assist farmers who have suffered a drought. We are, indeed, a very generous people. Should we not make it possible for all of our peoples to hold their heads high and to work and take care of their own needs, to feed themselves, and clothe themselves, and provide for themselves decent housing? Should we not make it possible for them to develop a free life in a free society without thinking always about their immediate survival?

My friends: God's Kingdom is about sharing. It is about a faith that is beyond ourselves; it is about a faith that looks, instead to God, our Father. God cares for us and calls us to a radically different life from the one that we would naturally live. He calls us to peace. He calls us to love our enemies. He calls us to share our last morsel with those who have not. He calls us to turn away from greed for wealth and lust for power and to seek first His Kingdom, His righteousness. Then we will know such an outpouring of peace and sharing that all the security sought by the Gentiles will be ours. He calls us, my friends, to a life more radical than any that we could possibly conceive, for He calls us to a Kingdom in which love rules and life is eternal. Amen.

John Walker's Christmas sermons were televised around the nation, and he received notes from people coast to coast who were moved by their simplicity and their profundity. In this sermon from Christmas 1987, he explores the theme of the Christ Child as a displaced person, using sophisticated biblical scholarship to establish the theological significance of the Christmas narrative cycle. Bishop Walker goes on to seamlessly translate the story of Christmas as a symbolic call for Christians everywhere to commit themselves to Christ and to Christ's ministry to the displaced persons of the world who wait for rebirth in Christ. Otherwise, he knew, the Christmas story has no real power to change lives.

The story of the birth of Jesus, as told in the Gospel of St. Luke, is a simple one. Mary, a young Jewish woman, is married to Joseph, a carpenter, and lives in Nazareth, and is about to give birth to her first child. Augustus Caesar, Emperor of Rome, has decreed there should be a census in all the world. Everyone had to return to his own city to be counted. So Joseph took Mary from Nazareth and returned to Bethlehem (the home of his forefathers) to be counted. While they were there, the time came for Mary to deliver. And she gave birth to her first born, a son, wrapped him in swaddling cloths and laid him in a manger because there was no place for them in the inn.

For our purposes, the important phrase is "there was no place for them in the inn." Although we recognize the legendary quality of this statement, we focus on it because it provides us with a key to understanding how the Church would later view this child, and because it is a theme mentioned in St. Matthew and St. John as well. Although they use different words, the thought is the same. There is in Matthew's account the threat to Jesus' life; the decree by Herod the King to put to death all male babies of a certain age and the flight to Egypt to save the infant's life. St. John, who is not concerned about biography, states it as the rejection of Jesus. He says, "He came unto his own and his own received him not."

Thus, whichever account we read, a certain picture emerges. In Luke, Jesus is seen as homeless because he is forced to be born in a cow's stall. In Matthew's account, he is a refugee moving quickly from place to place to fulfill prophecy or to escape death; and in John he is rejected. All of these accounts have profound meaning. They project a picture of a rejected Jesus; a king without a country or a home—certainly without a palace. It is likely, however, that he was only temporarily homeless. While he was probably not a refugee, circumstances do lead us to see him as a displaced person.

We are left with a dilemma. Is he a king, or even special? Or is he an ordinary child from an ordinary family? We must decide. And our decision will be based on what fits with the character of his life and ministry. The exact circumstances of his birth are important only insofar as they reveal something about the kind of person he was to be. As the legends indicate, and as both St. Mark and St. John demonstrate in their gospels, the suppositions about his birth are unimportant except as they tie Jesus back to Moses; back to David through Bethlehem; or are pointing to his future life and ministry, in which he will focus on those least able to care for themselves.

But whether we see Jesus as homeless, or as a displaced person, we must see him as being different from the moment of his birth. He had a home no doubt in Bethlehem or Nazareth. He had his parents who were not affluent by any standard. He seems to have had few worldly possessions except the bare necessities. His life would lead to a ministry of concern for the poor, the homeless, and the displaced. All that Matthew and Luke say about him suggests a difference between his and the ordinary life. Take, for example, his later appearance in the Temple where he is questioned by the Elders and Scribes. He would gather a following and ask them to give up everything to follow him. He would say to the rich young man, that even though you have kept the law you lack compassion, so go sell all of your goods, give the proceeds to the poor, and come and follow me.

Jesus founded a religious community that would be different from most others because it would concentrate its energies not on possessions, but on people; claiming their hearts, their minds, and their bodies. Later, he would claim their souls as well. He would ask that community to provide for the world a witness to his ministry of reconciliation and peace, by reaching out to the poor and the sick, to the homeless and the oppressed.

Some of you might ask where this is heading. Are we to have yet another exhortation on the sins and failures of mankind? Why not just tell the story of Christmas in all of its simplicity and magic? Why do we have to talk about hunger, oppression, or displaced persons on Christmas morning?

To answer in detail or with statistics would take too long and would serve no useful purpose. But you are right to ask! This is, after all, a day of joy for millions of people around the world. But, these questions are always raised by the story of Jesus' birth because they are intrinsic to that story. The coming of the Messiah that many believed was imminent, was to be a day of deliverance and a day of joy. A new age was to come that would bring revolutionary change in human nature, and God's laws would be honored. Wars would cease, thieves would change their ways, greed would disappear, mankind would have a second chance. For two-thousand years, the Church on this day would deliver sermons about God's love, Christ's peace, and the salvation of mankind.

The Church, however, even in its greatest euphoria would have to remind itself that in order for the new age to come into being, the old had to be overcome, done away with, destroyed. Did his birth bring true reconciliation to the peoples of the earth? Then oppression had to be removed from the human landscape. Was life to be healthful and fulfilling? Then sin and sickness had to be overcome. Did the coming of the Messiah mean new life? Then death had, somehow, to be abolished.

The experience of the community of Christ teaches us that there was no magic involved in God's intervention in the affairs of his people. The Messiah's birth would not see an immediate transformation of life on earth. At no time soon would the lion and the lamb cohabit. Men, neither then nor now, would beat their swords into plowshares or abolish forever the weapons of war and death. The Messiah was not to be God's magic wand to accomplish what we neither could nor would do ourselves.

The ministry of Jesus reveals that although God was and is always present with us, those whom he created would have to continue to make hard decisions. Neither oppression nor sickness are abolished because we wish it so. Nor do love, justice, peace, or reconciliation come gift wrapped under a tree. These things are bought by the determination of men and women to build a better world. They are paid for by the death of millions who comprise the suffering of every age.

Jesus was born a helpless infant. At the moment of his birth he does not have a house or even a room. He may even have been a displaced person. Certainly there were others like him. But he would grow up to become a teacher, a rabbi, a priest of God. Drawing on the events surrounding his own birth and childhood, he would carry on a ministry that emphasized his deep concern for peace; for the hungry; the sick and the homeless; for the oppressed and the dying. In the end he would weep for those who remained; whose task was to be partners in the building of his Kingdom. He promised to be with them (and us!) even unto the end of the ages. He sent the Holy Spirit to be God with us—to be Christ with us—guiding us as teacher and comforter to strengthen our work.

The difference between his world and ours is that there are millions of babies being born today for whom there is no room in the inn. The number of refugees created since World War II is so great that whole nations could be formed with them. In any city the thousands who qualify as displaced persons remind us that, although the Messiah has come, there is still work for us to do, to respond to those who come seeking God's Kingdom.

Millions of Americans who claim the name of Christ surrounded by affluence, will celebrate this birth with joy, and renewed hope of salvation. Millions of others who do not believe will celebrate because even those whose faith is known to God alone apparently need something in which to rejoice, something to celebrate, something even perhaps of the "magic"—the silent night, the star that guides, the warmth of the manger where even nature bows and celebrates.

However, for this Holy Day to have meaning and effectiveness, there needs also to be the firm belief that God lives and that he loves us so much that he will never desert us. Once a long time ago he sent the Messiah. Now God will forever send the Holy Spirit as promised by his Christ. It is our commitment to that Christ and to His promise of salvation that makes the Christmas Story have power in our lives. It is by following him that we remember the millions who like him are rejected or displaced, seeking a place to be born or reborn in the Christ.

It is good that we rejoice and celebrate, but it is also good to remember whose birth it is we celebrate and in which we rejoice, because intrinsic to that birth and our acceptance of it, is our own death and resurrection to a new life of grace and to a ministry of reconciliation. Amen.

Chapter 7

The Heart of Downtown

A city set on a hill cannot be hid.—Matthew 5:14

John Walker was a man of the city. In a 1978 address
to the graduating class of Virginia Seminary, he said so
himself:

> I am a city person, born in the city, in poverty. I was
> educated in the city. When I came to Virginia
> Seminary from Detroit in 1951, I felt that for the
> first time in my life I was living in the country. I
> have worked almost all of my life in the city. I am
> knowledgeable of how cities work. It is there that I
> have my being. When I am away from the city I
> become fearful. Country noises such as cows
> bawling in the dark frighten me. I long for the
> comfortable sounds of the city—police sirens, fire
> engines, cars racing, and people walking. I am
> steeped in the city's mystique.

It was in the city that he found his calling and exercised
his most significant ministry. It was the city he lived for
and died in.

It was with some relief that Walker returned to the
city of Washington in 1966 after a decade in the New
Hampshire countryside. It was, for him, a modern day
Jerusalem and Rome, a city set upon a hill. Actually,
several hills, as he pointed out, as he sought ways to make
his post as Canon Missioner relevant to inner-city

Washington: Capitol Hill, seat of national political power; "University Hill," home of Catholic University and nearby Howard University, symbols of the nation's need for educated citizens; Arlington Hill, brooding over what he called "the squandered lives of our young men," courageous, determined, proud, but nonetheless testimony to the arrogance and folly of those who may know how to win the war but always lose the peace; and Mt. St. Alban, rising above them all, at the time a yet-unfinished reminder of the religious heritage of the nation.

It was, and is, a divided city, rent in half by two rivers and Rock Creek: one part the home of the world's most powerful people; the other, home to some of the nation's poorest. John Walker knew and loved both sides. His portfolio was fairly open-ended, as he reminded Dean Sayre in his first annual report on his work as Canon Missioner. His task, "to expand the Cathedral's ministry to the Washington community and to the nation," he interpreted as an opportunity to experiment responsibly by immersing himself in "the great problems that people face as they live in this nation which increasingly becomes a nation of cities."

Among those problems, Walker identified the following ones as special concern and interest: poverty, crime, education, and race. To address them, he organized special services, put on conferences large and small, gave special sermons and talks. He served on task forces and boards, wrote reports, and appeared on radio and TV. He played a major role in the Cathedral's association with a drug treatment center organized by the Black Men's Development Center. He made a name for himself as a speaker and conference leader, as a black man who could help white people understand the Civil Rights Movement. He supported black artists and black students. He advised foreign visitors about race relations in the United States, and he advised U.S. diplomats what to say about the American race problem overseas. All told, in 1970 alone, he chalked up almost 100 events and institutions with which he was involved (a number, he wrote Dean Sayre, that represented a "curtailment of activities" that had been interfering on the time he spent on direct ministry at or for the Cathedral; over half of his community activities he undertook on his days off).

By 1975, Walker was a noted Washington personality, largely thanks to the development of his own television show ("Overview," shown on WRC-TV from 1970–1977). The show became an extension of his ministry and his primary concerns. The title of the first episodes make that clear: "The Church and the City" (The cathedral invites four citizens to discuss the involvement of the Church in important concerns of the city, including Home Rule and public education); "The Cathedral Culture from the City" (African Heritage Dancers and Drummers and Mother Scott, soul gospel singer); "The Cathedral, the Church, and Social Responsibility" (Drug care programs, war and peace, law enforcement and individual rights). The program never degenerated into a commercial for the Cathedral and its programs, thanks to Walker's vigilance. He resisted programs on the cathedral's liturgical music, buildings, and flowers. He wanted the Cathedral to be seen not as a fortress of propriety on Mt. St. Alban, but rather as a force in the federal city.

As his work load increased, and as the prospect of his election as diocesan bishop loomed, Walker agreed to immerse himself in the nitty-gritty details of the life of the District of Columbia's internal governance. He became a member of the Citizen's Advisory Council to the Chief of Police. He served on a task force charged with examining the problem of judicial tenure, a hot political topic in the District in the mid 1970s. Within months, Walker would become Bishop Coadjutor and find himself in the center of national church politics as well.

In February 1977, Walker was one of fifteen bishops who met in Chicago to reflect theologically on the crisis facing urban America. They were also reflecting fiscally. Big money was at stake as the Episcopal Church moved forward with its plans to launch a $100 million fund-raising drive to fund mission projects throughout the United States. The appeal was potentially enormously controversial, with many more conservative churchmen of the opinion that it represented a thinly-veiled attempt by social-action-oriented bishops to further embroil the Church in political matters that lay beyond its main area of concern. But as the new "Venture in Mission" campaign began, bishops like John Walker were afraid that the money would not address the Church's mission in the city.

In a letter to then Presiding Bishop John M. Allin, the bishops made their objective clear:

> Our Church must give high priority to a pastoral, servant ministry on behalf of the people victimized by our deteriorating cities—many of these people black, Hispanic, and poor—and it must also give high priority to a Christian assault on the social systems and economic forces which have led us to create not the biblical image of the heavenly city but a reality that breeds crime, oppression, poverty and hopelessness.

To advance this agenda, the Urban Bishops Coalition was formed. Its first chairman was John Walker, under whose leadership the Coalition developed formal action strategies and made a thoroughgoing and eloquently reasoned request for $12.5 million of Venture in Mission funds to help end the arms race, promote community economic redevelopment, improve industrial relations, revitalize parish ministry, enlarge the Church's outreach to minorities, ease the strains between police and their communities, and oppose capital punishment.

The Urban Bishops Coalition formed educational seminars, held public hearings, lobbied Congress, created partnerships with social justice movements, and met with White House officials. The group helped bring into being a broader organization of clergy and laity concerned about the plight of cities, the Episcopal Urban Caucus. The Coalition worked at the Church's national level to help design and promote Jubilee Ministries, a clearinghouse and support structure for grassroots social action ministries that by 2002 included nearly 500 projects in urban areas across the United States and Central America. Modeling their activity after the Catholic Church's American episcopacy, the Coalition issued a Labor Day Pastoral letter in 1982, printed in the *New York Times*. Further reflection led to a major statement of applied theology that was ultimately endorsed by the House of Bishops as a document worthy of study by the entire Church.

This document, known in its revised version as "Economic Justice and the Christian Conscience," comprises nearly 1000 lines of text that range from biblical exegesis, to economic analysis, to social critique. In essence, it examines the question of why severe poverty exists in the midst of prosperous western capitalist democracies. It pronounces judgment on injustices like the increasing gap between the rich and the poor; the failure of nations to feed and provide medical care for poor children; the lack of educational assistance for postsecondary education; and the inability of displaced workers to find systematized retraining programs. It reaffirms the Urban Bishops Coalition's pro-union stance. It calls for parishes to stand with the poor by intimately interacting with them in their neediness while at the same time studying and seeking to correct the systemic causes of poverty. The document's main prescription, however, is for a fundamental realignment of social values that places people above the needs of production, a reforming path that the paper recognizes will be marked by "lively public debate, political confrontations, and certainly some redistribution of wealth." The Church, the report concludes, will be forced to address corporate and individual avarice, become strategically informed about economic justice issues, and work for effective government intervention.

In the midst of complicated questions about full employment, labor-management relations, and capitalist theory, bishops like John Walker boiled the issue down to this simple yet profound statement: "We could, if we wished, refashion our American life so as to produce a decent life for all."

At its height, about two-thirds of the House of Bishops was involved in one way or another with the Urban Bishops Coalition and its initiatives. It was an impressive witness to John Walker's extraordinarily effective leadership, both on a personal and on an institutional level. His work in urban ministry provides perhaps the best example of how he accomplished so much. The way he worked remains instructive. Bishop Walker's concern for urban ministry was grounded in thoughtful biblical reflection and solid theological thinking. It took seriously secular and religious scholarship on urbanization and related topics, and anchored itself in a clear understanding of the Church's and the nation's history.

His working style was a model for bishops and other executive decision makers in the Church. He shared his mind and expertise over the years, a sort of informal consultation service for ecclesiastic policymakers. His advice was well-respected by people in authority throughout the Episcopal Church.

In amazing ways, John Walker combined a thoroughly personal approach to problem solving with a thoroughgoing understanding of complex organizations and their dynamic structures. A front-page incident that occurred in 1979 illustrates the point.

The story is unsettlingly reminiscent of several other, more recent events. It painfully illustrates the shocking lack of progress society has made since John Walker's death and the urgency with which the Church must continue to address the issues on which his ministry focused. The incident began with an African-American insurance salesman named Arthur McDuffie, a 33-year-old Miami resident with an expired driver's license out for a ride on his cousin's motorcycle. It was a warm December night when he ran a red light and became the object of a high-speed police chase through the city's streets. At speeds of up to 100 m.p.h., officers pursued him, perhaps even fired their weapons at him, until he slowed down and, some say, said, "I give up."

When he stopped, a number of policemen—ten or more—threw him off the motorcycle and took turns beating him to death with their flashlights and night clubs. After smashing in his skull like a cracked egg, they considered breaking his legs. They used a squad car to run over his motorcycle; and, they filed false reports stating that Mr. McDuffie had been injured in a traffic accident. He died four days later.

After Christmas at home with his family, one of the

officers involved suffered enough remorse to tell the truth, launching an investigation that led to the sensational trial of four white policemen. The prosecutor was Janet Reno, later to become the Attorney General of the United States.

Five months and a change of venue after the crime, an all-white jury acquitted all the officers, and Miami erupted into the worst civil disturbance in U.S. history: more than 1,100 people arrested, 18 people dead (including several women and children), $80 million of property destroyed, and business damaged and lost in excess of $200 million. The flames burned for three nights. Miami was declared a federal disaster area. Within days, the government had launched a sweeping investigation of the Miami-Dade County police department.

Within days, John Walker and his associates were speaking on behalf of the Urban Bishops Coalition and its daughter organization, the Episcopal Urban Caucus. Walker worked to mobilize the Church's resources, supporting the Bishop's (The Rt. Rev. Calvin Schofield of Southeast Florida) request for emergency funds to alleviate his people's suffering, by writing the Presiding Bishop. He made contact with Bishop Schofield, offering support and expressing hope that the Church could work to "ameliorate the conditions which produced the anger and frustration which called forth the violence." He coordinated the response of Cathedral Canon Lloyd Casson, Chair of the Caucus, in a letter-writing campaign to the Justice Department and to officials in Florida. They called for investigation and reporting, like everyone else. But they also called for the building of trust, for the empowerment of the economically oppressed, for the redress of inequality, for the creation of hope through action.

John Walker had a heart for suffering people, and he had a head that knew how to change the world not only to alleviate their suffering, but fundamentally to restructure the social circumstances that led to their suffering in the first place. Such informed, articulate, pastoral politicians are rare indeed.

It was Walker's goal to inspire others to take up his mission to the city. In 1978 he spoke of it to the students and faculty of his alma mater's Missionary Service. Each year Virginia Seminary celebrates its rich evangelical heritage of sending its sons and daughters around the world to spread the Gospel. Walker came to remind the Church's leaders that they could not ignore Boston, Hartford, Baltimore, Providence, New York, Newark, Philadelphia, Pittsburgh, Washington, Detroit, Chicago, St. Louis, Nashville, Birmingham and the rest, that the mission of the Church in the coming decades was to recreate the cities of this nation as the City of God.

Armed with competent social analysis and careful economic research, Walker called for bold action in the city and explained how he thought such action could be accomplished in the Church:

> It is *the cities* that are the repositories of the poor and of the most acutely damaged victims of the systemic economic, political, and social malfunctioning of the society. This is where our mission must begin...
>
> So many are crippled by the horrible consequences of joblessness and hunger; by alcoholism and drug addiction; by social and economic injustice and by racist policies; by classism and sexism; homelessness and rootlessness; by neglect and oppression; and hopelessness and despair.
>
> The aim of the Coalition is primarily to serve as a reminder to the church of what our mission is.

Standing on the cutting edge, unencumbered by bureaucracies, we *pledge* to hold before the church the awful challenges and tremendous opportunities to which God calls us in the urban mission.

It is hard to imagine our being able to take steps too radical or too drastic for the circumstances. Rather, we need to fear a too *timid* approach...

Even with our present state of awareness—with so much more to learn—it is clear that any response we may make which is less than serious will reveal a gross insensitivity to the plight of those people we are called to serve.

And a part of being serious means a willingness to make hard, inconvenient decisions and radical readjustments to our present ways of doing things.

It was precisely this radical readjustment for which John Walker lived and died. He worked it out and called it forth from others in fear and trembling, with gentleness, humor, and steely-eyed resolve. He became a living bridge between the hills of Washington, crossing the great divide over Rock Creek Park, spanning with ease the gulf between the Capital and the Anacostia.

In an appreciation published in the *Washington Post* just after Walker's death, the former president of Georgetown University, Fr. Timothy Healy, wrote,

> ...He knew in his bones the irreducible gap between the cuckoo in Washington's nest—the federal establishment—and the real city. Both of us feared being locked up in the cuckoo's half of the nest, with its banks and lawyers, lobbyists, think tanks, and universities. He ached over how separate the intellectual and social life of the capital was from the lives and pains of the people who make it work, who in their poverty hold it together with wiring and roads, shops and stores, with service and

humor and hard work...

He could move from [affluent] Northwest [Washington, D.C.] to [poverty-stricken] Southeast without changing smile or rhythm...as if both halves over 10 square miles were bonded somehow in his own person.

So they were.

John Walker imagined they should be in every Chief Pastor, urban or rural, black or white, because he foresaw that the destiny of the nation lies with its cities and with the Church's commitment to serving them. He concluded one of his last sermons at the consecration of a bishop with a prayer that scans like the poetry he knew and loved so well:

> Pray often, my brother. Sing when you can. Daily weep over the city and wash the feet of the weak and lowly, the black and white, the poor and the rich, the sick and the healthy, the believer and those who do not yet believe. Be consecrated in truth, and be one with all in the Lord. Amen.

In recognition of his work in founding the Interfaith Council of Greater Washington, Bishop Walker was invited to address the National Press Club in 1979. His wide-ranging speech examined ecumenical relations, the history of racism in the United States, separation of Church and State, and the role of religious institutions in modern society. He began, however, with this moving account of a visit to Detroit, his childhood home. His experience there became an important point of reference for his remarks; they speak eloquently of his concern for the city.

It is an honor to have been invited here to address the National Press Club. I wish that I could also claim it is a pleasure. But it is not a pleasure. It once might have been, but that was in the days when words had meaning, when ideas possessed force, and action grew out of those words and ideas. We stand at the moment on the half-deserted streets of a culture remembering a time that was and longing—not nostalgically for the past, but tragically for a lost culture.

A short time ago, a fund-raising trip (that bane of every educator, Churchman, and all who serve in non-profit institutions) took me to Detroit, a city of memories in which I had come to manhood. My eight-year-old son was with me and had asked me to show him the neighborhood of my early years, the school where I first learned, and the house I had called home. I did so with fear—fear that I'd be overwhelmed by memories. Never-believing in half-way measures, I decided to wallow in nostalgia for a little while, to immerse myself in memories and maybe even to shed a tear for the past. So we drove—first East along the river and then halfway across the river on the bridge, a park of surprising beauty...a park where people of many races and nationalities were driven by heat waves in the 1930s, seeking a breeze or a breath of air. Fans were useless, and air conditioning yet unheard of. In the summer of 1979, the park was nearly empty and somewhat seedy. The yachts were there in the marina and the Children's Zoo (a reminder of better days). My son was unimpressed, so we headed North along Grand Boulevard, past the public library and what had once been the stately homes of the very rich. Now they were run-down publishing houses, florists, funeral homes and the like. A left turn on Charlevoix, a name left over from the French past, and suddenly, we were there.

The house still stood, but just barely. The faces of strangers laughed on street corners; the school had survived, but looked unnecessarily small. The once-huge playground where Joe Louis would come to thrill us with his presence, was filled now with debris, not children. Quickly we fled back downtown where new life seemed clinging to the bridge to Windsor, Ontario, where civilization and culture seemed alive and well.

That brief excursion into the past produced two feelings: one of nostalgia, the other of despair, or as the great Danish theologian Søren Kierkegaard would have called it, deep, deep dread. These two feelings were summed up for me that day by a song and a poem. I could almost hear the voice of Frank Sinatra singing: "Time was, when we had fun on schoolyard swing, and we exchanged graduation rings, one lonely yesterday. Time was, when we wrote love letters in the sand, we lingered over our coffee and, dreaming the night away. Picnics and hayrides and midwinter sleigh rides, and never apart. Hikes in the country, and there's more than one tree..." This, nostalgia, warm and smothering, lovely and dreamy nostalgia. Names come back. There were Italian (Benvenite), German (Heitman), French (LaDuke), Lebanese, Irish, England, Polish, Scottish, Syrian, Greek,

Native American, Chinese—a truly American community, diverse, but unified in their diversity.

But nostalgia isn't all. There was, as I said, a deep sense of despair bordering on dread. And out of that sense of dread, the words of Thomas Sterns Eliot came repeatedly:

> Let us go then, you and I...
> Let us go, through certain half-deserted streets
> The muttering retreats
> Of restless nights...
> Streets that follow like a tedious argument
> Of insidious intent
> To lead you to an overwhelming question
> Do not ask, "What is it?"

The sense of dread is occasioned by the realization that where we now stand is not in the area of nostalgia, which merely comes about because we change—life changes, time passes. Rather we stand in the presence of deep cultural change, change so great that we might be justified in saying that we are witnessing the death of culture. Nor is this the first time this has happened. It happened in the fifth-century A.D. when Christianity took over the dying Roman Empire, and though it continued to live for a time in new forms, very gradually, the old culture disappeared, except for a few structures, ruins of the past, fit only for historical study.

The death of this western culture (some say) began with the Industrial Revolution and is culminating in the fulfillment of the technological revolution in which we currently live. (Others might place the beginning at an earlier time, but no matter.) The death of this culture is seen in the loss of credibility of every major institution in Western life... To what do we attribute this loss of credibility?

I am convinced that the basic problem in Western and more specifically American life is what might be called the lack of coincidence between the principles, precepts, or axioms of a Christian/democratic society and that society's behavior or action...

The government, the Courts, businesses, education, the laws, and medicine have all reflected the suppression of the people of color in this land. All of this was sanctioned by the religious institutions. And that great guardian of public honesty—the press—found itself suffering from moral laryngitis when it came to addressing the grievances of Native Americans, blacks, and all other minorities. Is it not strange that until the Civil Rights Movement became powerful, it was easier for gangsters with Anglo-Saxon names to buy homes anywhere than for blacks, Hispanics, Jews, Native Americans, or any person of color, no matter how decent or honorable?

Given all these facts, it is not surprising that some day the young and others would rise up against these institutions that talked peace and practiced war, that talked love and practiced hate, that talked the pursuit of happiness and practiced job discrimination. Is it any wonder that credibility would suffer in religious institutions that worshipped a God who is perceived as being concerned about the poor, the oppressed, and the imprisoned, and at the same time added to their poverty, their oppression, and their imprisonment?

Chapter 8

Children of Cush

And they shall be afraid and ashamed of Ethiopia.—Isaiah 20:5

> *Uganda is a beautiful country, with gentle hills and lovely valleys. But it is also a lonely place.*
>
> *Sitting here at Tucker College we might almost be in another country. Our life is outwardly not too different from that at home. The rooms are like any in the western world; there is an icebox that makes ice, a small washing machine, nice cabinets.*
>
> *Outside there is another world, or maybe it is better to say two or three worlds. There is the world of the uneducated African who doesn't quite understand this industrialized and somewhat mechanized society into which he has been plunged by events.*
>
> *Also there is the world of the educated African who would like to see this a true nation able to handle its own affairs without European or American help, but knowing at the same time that he is closer to the European and the American than he is to those Africans who are fresh out of the bush.*
>
> *Finally, there are the Europeans and Americans living in our insecure little world, fearful lest at any moment we are sent packing. Most are here to be helpful, but I suspect that not many know how.*

So John Walker wrote in his journal less than a month after arriving for the first time in Africa. It was the fall of 1964. After a hectic summer of traveling to be with family and friends, the young scholar-priest had landed with his

JOHN WALKER—A MAN FOR THE 21ST CENTURY

wife and infant son in Mukono, Uganda at the Bishop
Tucker Theological College for a year's assignment of
leading the choir, assisting with services in local churches
and missions, heading the communal work program, and
teaching Old Testament, English, and Church History to
a handful of indigenous men seeking ordination in the
Anglican Church of East Africa. He wrote home to tell of
condescending bishops, dedicated missionaries, a child
with chickenpox, a young wife smiling and nodding as if
she understood the animated gossip of native women
around her sewing table.

He wrote of magnificent African scenery, of terrify-
ing journeys on local roads, and of more than a few very
large, very poisonous snakes. But mostly what John
Walker wrote about Africa had to do with its people, with
whom he fell in love. Even as he became more and more
responsible for the administration of a large diocese and
ever more deeply concerned with affairs of the national
church, his heart beat for Africa. He became a driving force
for African development and relief. He trained African
bishops and paid for new Prayer Books and Hymnals
when theirs had begun to fall apart. He became a player
in the corporate world, influencing policy and facilitating
individual philanthropy. He protested against apartheid
and gave Desmond Tutu a high-profile American religious
forum for his pleas to end racial injustice in South Africa.
He sparred with Senators, conservatives and liberals alike,
and made headline news when he broke with the accepted
liberal stance with regard to corporate disinvestment in
Pretoria.

Unlike the many people (of whom he wrote in his
1964 journal) who wanted to be helpful to Africa but
could not be, John Walker found out how. He did it by
listening to Africa's people. While other missionaries made
students wait silently at the entrance to their comfortable

compounds until someone noticed they were there, Walker left his every Thursday night and went to eat at his students' homes, where they laughed together because he had such trouble chewing the tough beef they served him and his family for dinner.

While some enjoyed the kowtowing of African women as they greeted men by walking toward them on their knees, Walker once told an African father that if he did not stop his daughters from humiliating themselves so, he would never visit that home again. (The greeting had been a test. He passed.) While some avoided greeting Africans at all because of the formalities that required you to exchange news about the health and activities of every living relative, Walker came to chuckle about and to cherish the church services that took an hour or more to get going.

John Walker felt at home in Africa, and he became a passionate advocate for Africa's people. It was fitting that he began his love affair with what the Old Testament called the "people of Cush" at the Bishop Tucker College in 1964. The place and time were right. The school was named after Alfred Tucker, first Bishop of Uganda. Tucker had been chosen to head the Anglican Church's mission to Equatorial Africa following the scandalous deaths of his two predecessors, one of whom was martyred on orders from the King of Buganda. Tucker ordained the region's first indigenous clergy in 1892 and began a Bible College for their education the following year. It is the sort of ministry John Walker would have had, had he been a Victorian missionary to Africa.

Uganda in the mid-1960s fit him better. It was a heady time for Uganda and those who lived there, following as it did fast on the heels of the country's independence from Great Britain and the enthronement of its first indigenous bishops. It was a good place for a twentieth century

African-American who was learning how to use his gifts as a leader among clergy and his savvy as a politician.

In all his work for Africa, Walker again demonstrated his deep and instinctual understanding of how effective leadership works. Guided by unwavering convictions, he moved with the extraordinary flexibility that is necessary to respond to the Spirit's movement. Still, Walker's overall approach to the problem of how best to help Africa reflects the approach he consistently followed to address complex issues and move them toward resolution.

The vast and complicated issues surrounding Africa and its relationship with the developed world leave most world leaders shaking their heads just before turning away. Aside from occasional guilt-ridden efforts at relief and the occasional fear of a communist uprising, much of the United States' approach to Africa during John Walker's lifetime was to ignore its existence. But Reverend-then Canon-then Bishop Walker threw himself wholeheartedly into making a real difference in the lives of thousands of people across the continent.

He began by listening to individuals, really listening. Next, he put in place a forum for systematically gathering information from people who could provide many points of view. He personally engaged key players, moving quickly to solidify and institutionalize the responses that emerged from the conversation. He guided newborn institutions as they expanded their mission and diversified their activities, promoting growth while providing a reference point for fidelity to its first cause. He raised funds energetically, spoke out forcefully, and skillfully drew attention to the cause. He was not afraid to ruffle feathers and go against the tide. He was known, occasionally, to change his mind.

As the U.S. racial upheavals of the 1960s began to recede, Walker began turning his attention to Africa. In the early 1970s he used *Overview*, his weekly television program, to talk with African bishops about life in South Africa and Uganda. In 1974 he became Chairman of the Board of Africare, a new nonprofit organization built from the ground up by American blacks dedicated to development and relief programs throughout Africa. He worked with the Presiding Bishop's Fund for World Relief to help alleviate the suffering of famine-stricken Ethiopia and Sudan. In 1981 he was instrumental in founding an ongoing training conference for new bishops in East Africa. He supported the conference financially through diocesan programs and budgets, and he taught in Kenya twice more (in 1983 and in 1989).

In 1984, Walker met Desmond Tutu, the outspoken South African Anglican bishop who had just been awarded the Nobel Peace Prize for his leadership in the nonviolent protest movement against apartheid. The two men became fast friends. Walker traveled to Tutu's enthronement as the Archbishop of Cape Town, and soon after, he moved into the most vocal phase of his advocacy for economic and social justice for South Africa's black majority.

It was a turbulent political era. As Reagan began his second term in 1985, budget deficits soared, and conservative senators Phil Gramm, Warren Rudman, and Earnest Hollings spearheaded legislation that capped U.S. spending, and as a consequence, gutted the foreign aid budget for Africa. The Reagan administration's policy of "constructive engagement" with South Africa was coming under increasing attack. Media coverage of atrocities in the South African homelands were intensifying in the wake of Tutu's post-Nobel visibility on the world stage. Never one to shrink from a battle against high-handed government, John Walker joined the fray. On March 13, Walker invited the people of his diocese to join him in protesting at the Embassy of South Africa. Almost one hundred of them did.

Walker cast his protest as no mere publicity stunt, but rather as a prophetic action of solidarity with his friend Desmond Tutu and a holy condemnation of the systemic evil that was threatening to silence Tutu and every other black South African.

> I submit that those who have not seen how black South Africans are treated may indeed misunderstand what we do here. I have been to South Africa. I've seen and heard the abuse heaped upon Christians, many of whom are members of the Anglican Communion. I am led, I trust, by our Lord Jesus Christ to bear witness in support of our Christian brothers and sisters in South Africa, who though created in the image of God, are treated as things and animals by other Christians. They live lonely and isolated lives. Frequently they must wonder if God cares for them at all.
>
> One of the ways God demonstrates his love for them is through us... I believe that my ministry as deacon, priest, and bishop in the Church of God demands that I show my love for the oppressed peoples of the world in some concrete, albeit in this, symbolic action.

Walker and some others were duly arrested, albeit symbolically. After a trip to the police station, where he joked with officers he knew from his days on the Chief's Advisory Council, the Bishop and his followers were released from custody.

The incident's meaning was complex. Some questioned Walker's tactics. One of his priests wrote to ask him what could possibly be accomplished by such a media event, a daily spectacle arranged by the political policy watchdog group Transafrica. The unwritten lines of motivation might also be open to more than one interpretation. The cynical might wonder who was using whom—prominent and media-savvy political leaders, celebrity causes, and ambitious clergy make for a volatile mix. (Walker's arrest came on the heels of the announcement that he was one of three final candidates in the coming election for Presiding Bishop.)

While he would not question Bishop Walker's motives, *Washington Times* editorial page editor William Cheshire did ask why no one had bothered to protest at the Soviet, Ethiopian, Nicaraguan, or Chinese embassies. At those compounds, protesters trespassing within 500 yards of the embassy would have been arrested for real. Cheshire's editorial, "Climbing the Ecclesiastical Flagpole: A Trendy Event for the Flock," accused Walker of seeking glory without pain. It featured a full-page caricature of the Bishop in his rochet and chimere, sitting and grinning on a platform atop a flagpole like some later-day Uncle St. Simon Stylites.

Within a year, greater controversy was to come. Through a process of personal reflection and dialog with South African blacks (and at least one clandestine meeting with an official of the ruling National Party), Walker ruffled the feathers of more than a few black liberals by speaking out against the policy of total American disinvestment in South Africa. By 1986, it had become politically correct for corporate America to protest apartheid by withdrawing capital from South African companies. Boards of directors raced to rid themselves of financial ties to companies that even indirectly supported apartheid by doing business with South Africa. U.S. companies began withdrawing in record numbers from the South African market, hoping to apply enough economic pressure to force the issue of reform.

Until 1986, Walker agreed that total disinvestment was the right path to follow, too. He led the Diocese of Washington and the National Cathedral as they both released resolutions in support of total disinvestment. On June 16th of that year, on the anniversary of the Soweto massacre, Bishop Walker announced in a *Washington Post* editorial that he had changed his mind.

At Virginia Theological Seminary and at the Church Pension Fund, two institutions among many on whose boards of directors he served, Walker voted against total divestment. (His vote at the seminary was a tiebreaker, and something of a surprise.) His argument was, in effect, an endorsement of forward thinking companies like General Motors. The multinational conglomerate car maker had not withdrawn from the South African market, but had rather agreed to abide by (or agreed only to invest in companies that abided by) a set of principles and timelines designed to support South African blacks while pressing for the repeal of apartheid. The principles had been proposed by the Rev. Leon Sullivan, noted African-American advocate for corporate responsibility and member of GM's board of directors, in 1977. However, by October 1986, GM was ready to give up on South Africa, too. The world's largest automobile manufacturer, and the largest employer of blacks in South Africa, announced it was leaving.

The decision made front-page news in the *Washington Post*, as did John Walker's personal campaign to oppose it. Having once argued for divestiture, Walker's mind was changed by first hand experience from two trips to South Africa in 1985. An editorial in the *Post* summarized his position:

> Bishop Walker believes that U.S. companies, rather than pulling out of South Africa and leaving that country to the winds of war, should provide more training for their black South African employees. His is a pragmatic approach to South Africa's problems—an approach he believes would lay the

groundwork for a peaceful transition to majority rule, while avoiding an economic collapse and its devastating effects on the nation's blacks.

It was a brave move of independence on Walker's part, one which immediately alienated him from a number of prominent civil rights organizations and one which set him in direct opposition to the official position of the National Church. In an extreme case of conscience making strange bedfellows, the Bishop found himself lauded in the editorial pages of the *Wall Street Journal*. The *Washington Times*, the capital's conservative daily paper, praised him for his "clear and pragmatic thinking," calling it the stuff of "true leadership."

In the final analysis, Walker had found the path of divestiture to be the means of cheap grace and painless self-righteousness of which he had been accused the year before after his symbolic arrest at the South African embassy. Instead, he argued,

> If we care about the people of South Africa, oppressed and oppressors alike, we must do the very hard, tedious, immediately unrewarding, hard work of staying put, assisting, cajoling, pushing, entreating, developing, promoting, providing, talking, and persuading that has to be done to keep South Africa in the mainstream of the world community...We must help keep them economically healthy, and we must be there with our companies to provide jobs, offer training, provide opportunities for advancement, decent housing for families, and health care systems as part of compensation. And, as those who care enough about that troubled land to be invested there in an uncertain climate, we must pressure, pressure, pressure for a recognition of the political and civil rights of all the people of South Africa.

For John Walker, it was a prophetic moment. Standing very much alone as a black man with clear civil rights credentials, and looking ahead to discern the future toward which others had not yet turned their imagination, he helped turn a reactionary tide—however much it may have been well-intentioned—into a realistic response toward injustice. He worked the problem from the inside, as he did all his life. If you don't stay, then you can't fight.

It was a lonely job. When John Walker looked at Africa, he saw loneliness. Perhaps it was his own, projected feeling. For all his pastoral skill and genuine love of people, Bishop Walker was a quiet man, introspective and frequently alone. He sat up late reading poetry and writing his own verse. He was still and deep.

He was like a bridge to Africa, both here and there at the same time, and yet not fully part of either: a black man in a white church, a poor man hobnobbing with the kings of industry and the holders of high office, American citizen and citizen of the developing world.

His thoughts often ran to Africa and her people. There were those who lived in the humidity and heat of the jungle, and those who dwelt within the cooling sight of Mt. Kenya. He was talking about them to one of his priests on September 14, 1989. Later that afternoon, he was stricken with the illness that set in motion a series of events that ended in his death. The business of the day ended, he made cups of tea and recalled the year he lived in Africa. He talked of his son, Tommy, playing among African children. It was the last appointment of his episcopal ministry. His heart turned to Africa.

This sermon from December 1986 contains Bishop Walker's profound reflections on the meaning of some of the Bible's most challenging literature and one of the Church's most demanding and misunderstood liturgical seasons. Here he equates the apocalyptic signs of the end of the world with the starving people of Africa; he sees in the oppressed blacks of South Africa both a coming judgment and an Advent invitation to find the presence of Christ in the midst of the world's suffering people.

The Old Testament lessons for Advent are often drawn from the Book of Isaiah, in large part from the prophecy referred to as Third Isaiah. Its words are similar to those used by the eighth century B.C. prophet whom we know as Isaiah. The words are even more similar to the cries of the psalmist and other prophets who lived some three hundred years later, at a time in Israel's history when the people of God were feeling abandoned and depressed. They cry out in sadness and anger. The portion of Isaiah appointed today is a psalm of lamentation. Israel is appealing to God to open the heavens and come down: "O that thou wouldst render, O that thou wouldst render heavens and come down to make thy name known to thy adversaries, and that the nations might tremble at thy presence."

Throughout much of the Old Testament, the psalmists and the prophets raise the same cry, "Come, make thyself known; show forth your power, crush the enemy, give to us your chosen people a sign of your approval, a sign of your mercy if we have sinned, a sign of your love for your people whom you call to be a special people, your very own people." This theme is picked up on by the Christian story, from its very beginning. Our season of Advent begins with the familiar hymn, "O, Come, O Come Emmanuel and ransom captive Israel that mourns in lonely exile here." Or this: "Come thou long expected

Jesus, born to set thy people free; from our fears and sins release us, let us find our rest in thee."

In every generation, men and women have longed for, cried out for, watched for God, for a Messiah to deliver them from oppression, from sin, from loneliness, fear of death, and from whatever burdens they may suffer. Universally they have tended to believe that if God were to come, that day would be a day of rejoicing, a day of victory, a day of hope realized. However, careful reading of the Old Testament or the New Testament reveals that both the prophets and the New Testament writers warn their people that the day of the Lord may be other than a day of joy and gladness.

Both Isaiah and St. Mark call upon the people to be on the watch for the coming of the Lord. Isaiah records it this way. "Upon your walls, O Jerusalem, I have set watchmen all the day and all the night and they shall never be silent." And this, in St. Mark's Gospel: "Take heed and watch, for you know not when the time will come." Or this: "Watch, therefore, for you know not when the master of the house will come." And, "What I say to you, I say to all," (to the whole Church, if you will): "Watch."

What Jesus is saying to his disciples and to all who will come after them is this: "Watch, for you do not know when God will come nor do really know what His coming will mean." Look for the signs. The watching always is related to the coming day of the Lord. Watch for His coming, look for the signs. The people of Israel were taught throughout their life in history that God—the Day of God—would come and he would judge the world on that day. They fully expected that when God arrived on the scene, His chosen people would be rewarded and their enemies put under them.

It was the prophet's job to tell the people that their expectations, their assumptions, were all wrong. They were waiting for the wrong thing, watching for the wrong signs. They had been misled, just as Jesus had foreseen when he warned his followers: "Take heed that no one leads you astray. Many will come in my name saying, 'I am he,' and they will lead many astray. And when you hear of wars and rumors of wars, do not be alarmed. This must take place, but the end is not yet. For nation will rise up against nation and kingdom against kingdom. There will be earthquakes in various places and there will be famines. This is but the beginning of the suffering." Those are not signs of triumph and reward. They are not the signs God's people were expecting. The day of the Lord, it turns out, will be more like a day of reckoning, a day of judgment for all people, including the people of God.

You will know when he is approaching. Read the signs. As we prepare in watchful waiting for the Savior's birth this Advent tide, how can we discern the signs that are before us? As we watch, how will we recognize Him when he appears? Perhaps it will be easier to say what the signs are not.

First, we should not expect to discover Him among the fancy, expensive gifts that we outdo each other in purchasing for our children and for others every Christmas.

Secondly, we shall not find Him in the tinsel and lights of the decorated Christmas trees, nor in the parties held to celebrate His birth. Thirdly, we shall not find him in the great feasts that are held each year, for increasingly these look more like the drunken, Roman revels which Christmas offsets.

Where then should we look? We are reminded of the words from that hymn, "Watchman tell us of the night, what its signs of promise are, traveler o'er yon mountains height, see that glory—beaming star. Watchman, does its beauteous ray, aught of joy or hope foretell? Traveler, yes; it brings the day, promised day of Israel."

The star is a sign.

But what does that star portend? Across the continent of Africa, we see millions of hungry, famine-ridden people marching across the desert. Are they following a star or are they merely looking for food? Do they seek a larger hope than they ever had before or do they expect to find new life? Whatever they seek, whatever they hope for, if we are seeking the savior which is Christ the Lord, the hungry marching people of Africa are a sign. If we read and look carefully, perhaps we will find Him there among these the least of His creation.

Or if we look to Poland, Nicaragua, or the Philippines—wherever men and women are seeking freedom, wherever they are experiencing terrorism and war. If we look carefully we may see his face in the face of a mother distorted by fear, of a child frightened and terrorized, of ambassadors or other persons in authority trembling before the tortures of those who have captured them. Or we may see him in the face of a dying soldier who at the moment of his reckoning seems to wonder what his death was for. Will we perchance see the Christ Child there?

Let us go back to Africa, the south, to Soweto, to Johannesburg, to the homelands, to a settlement where men live without their wives, where men live broken and lonely lives, without hope, frightened of the power that is lorded over them; to men who provide cheap labor for a Christian government, men who provide cheap labor for Christian businessmen; nay, rather slave labor to a Christian minority; to a place where people are held without trials, where leaders disappear or die mysteriously. Is this perhaps what Jesus meant when He said, "They will come who will lead you astray." Look carefully. Watch the faces. Among those downtrodden, you may see the face of the Savior who is Christ the Lord.

But one need not go as far afield as Africa, or Nicaragua, or the Philippines. Visit the hospitals in your own community. Visit those who are facing death from incurable diseases. Visit the mental hospitals, prisons, walk the streets of our cities and find the homeless people and look into their faces. Go into any place on this planet or in this land where people cling to life with little hope, with frightened, lonely faces. Can you discern Christ in those faces? What about those in prison, living on death row, doomed to die for their sins. Is Christ among them? He saved a thief on the cross. Will he also save these?

Finally (and this brings it home to all of us), follow the hearse and the loved ones to the graveside, to the very pit of hopelessness. Is he to be found there, this Christ? Of course he is—where else should he be? Christ, born in the grave, always in the grave. Christ, born in the back alleys of our towns and cities, born in the desert where famine lingers, in Ethiopia, in Chad, in Uganda, wherever people die of hunger; born in the prisons of despair, born on the death rows of every state and nation; born in the cancer ward; born in the hearts of those doomed to die in the wars born of politics; born in the hearts of those who grieve.

The One for whom we watch for as King and Savior does not surprise us. He sends signs in the sun and the moon and the stars; in the distress of nations, in earthquakes, fires, floods, and famines; in wars, disease, and death. Wherever humankind suffers, that is where we will find Him.

Watch, look, pray. For the Lord Christ cometh unto us. "O come, O come Emmanuel, and ransom captive Israel that mourns in lonely exile here, until the Son of God appear."

In this 1984 Easter greeting to the faithful, Bishop Walker writes of his growing respect and personal acquaintance with Desmond Tutu, who had increasingly become the international spokesman for black South Africans' protests against apartheid. The following year, Tutu would be enthroned as Archbishop of Cape Town, and at his invitation, John Walker and twelve others from the Episcopal Church were granted visas to attend the ceremony.

Tutu personally drove Walker to his hotel in Johannesburg. It was a seminal experience that would help to frame Walker's participation in the growing anti-apartheid movement in the United States.

Recently, it was my good fortune to be in the presence of a great friend and deeply committed Christian Churchman from the Republic of South Africa. He is the Right Reverend Desmond Tutu, formerly Dean of Johannesburg and Bishop of Lesotho. Presently he serves as the Secretary General of the South African Council of Churches. I had been notified that Bishop Tutu would be here for a series of meetings on Capitol Hill with the Assistant Secretary for African Affairs in the United States State Department.

I had not seen Bishop Tutu since the Lambeth Conference at Canterbury in 1978. However, he has been in the news a good bit of late having moved from a reconciling stance to a more aggressive one in regard to the separation of the races in his home country. In recent months he has had his passport lifted and found himself in jail for a minor act of opposition to government policy. He is, as a Christian, an outspoken critic of his government in its often terroristic acts against the black majority who live without freedom and without hope in that land. He is a man of courage who speaks the truth, always in love, wherever he may be and at whatever cost.

Bishop Tutu came to the United States to persuade our government not to change its longstanding policy of opposing apartheid. He further appealed to our President through the State Department not to invite the President of South Africa here for an official visit. Such an act would undercut the continuing efforts of the Anglican Church of South Africa in its battle against the oppressive measures practiced in that country. It would give aid and comfort to a government that is committed to the control of the black majority by whatever means available. The acts of terror against and the officially sanctioned murders of African leaders are documented. It is demoralizing to South African Christians such as Bishop Tutu—and ought to be to Christians here—that a U.S. Administration that has campaigned under the Christian banner can now seriously consider extending the hand of friendship to Prime Minister Botha and other officials from South Africa.

Quite apart from the impact on the lonely Anglican Church of South Africa, and quite apart from the destruction of hope that this would bring to black people everywhere, any effort to characterize the government of South Africa as a friend sends a signal to the so-called American Nazi Party and the Ku Klux Klan that the new America is open territory for the venom which they peddle across the land and that the new Administration will sanction their *right* to do so.

Some will argue that we are too easily alarmed, that such fears are exaggerated and, therefore, unwarranted. Perhaps so. On the other hand, it was a silent church in Germany and the world that encouraged the rise of Adolph Hitler, which led finally to the excesses which produced the Holocaust. Adolph Hitler paraded across Europe as an Anti-Communist. Would we today embrace him as a friend and ally?

I do not suggest that the government of South Africa is to be equated with Nazi Germany in 1945, but I do believe it to be traveling the same road. And it is possible, given a strong uprising of black South Africans to see a similar "final solution" coming into play.

Desmond Tutu has decided to stand against his government. He believes that it is what our Lord would have him do. I support him in this resolve. Before long he may join the long list of Christian martyrs who date from the first century to the recent regime of Idi Amin in Uganda. We are now into the season of Easter and Resurrection but for many of our brothers and sisters the world over it is in human terms an Easter devoid of hope. It may be that Lent for them will have to continue through a long dark night of struggle before the hope of Christ is again visible. I pray that we will pray with and for them and beyond that, that we will stand with them against all the forces of darkness that seek to destroy hope. In this world, we will know darkness and tribulation, but we remain of good hope for Christ *is* Risen and He *has* overcome the world.

Every ten years, the Archbishop of Canterbury invites bishops from throughout the Anglican Communion to join him for the Lambeth Conference. In 1988, Bishop Walker attended and quickly assumed a role of informal but substantial leadership. In this "Letter from Canterbury," he explains to his diocese the new realities of the Anglican Churches around the world. He ends it with an assessment that, for a man like John Walker, is characteristically optimistic. When many saw (and in fact continue to see) a future of conflict and schism, he saw the possibility of a better world.

Dear Friends,

As I write this we are beginning our third and last week at Canterbury. It seems, in fact, a much longer time since I left Washington. I suppose this is due in large part to the fact of the General Convention immediately preceding the trip here. Because so much of the subject matter is the same it is sometimes difficult to separate the details of the two.

The Lambeth Conference began 121 years ago at Lambeth Palace (the London residence of the Archbishop of Canterbury). At the first Lambeth Conference there were 30 or so bishops present, from the United Kingdom, Canada, and the U.S. At Lambeth 1988 there are some 525 bishops from around the world. From the American Church alone there are 130 bishops. From the African continent there are some 175. Add to these the bishops of Australia, Canada, the West Indies, Central America, South America, Indian Ocean, Melanesia and the Far East, and Archbishop Runcie's words "the Anglican Communion is no longer English," become an awesome reality.

Altogether more than 400 of the bishops of the Anglican Communion come from outside Great Britain and Ireland. Of these 525, more than 300 are of non-

English and non-European background. Again, the Archbishop of Canterbury is right in saying that the Lambeth Conference is no longer Anglo-Saxon.

What has this radical shift meant for the structure of Lambeth and for the concerns addressed? In the ten years since Lambeth 1978, the leadership of groups has shifted away from England to the non-English provinces. In every case the Bible study and small groups leadership has had to be shared with non-English bishops. For example, Group B in the Christianity and Social Order work group—the Bible study leader was from the U.S., the work group leader from Sudan, and the section leaders from England and South Africa. Of these four, three were black and one English. This pattern generally held through all the groups.

The importance of these statistics is seen in the fact that the agendas of the third world provinces tended to be different from those of the Western or "first world" provinces. For example, England's primary concerns were the issues of the ordination of women as priests and bishops, and ecumenical concerns. The concerns of the African, West Indian, and South American (as well as the U.S.) provinces were such matters as human rights, apartheid, poverty, world food supply, third world debt, AIDS, refugees, and peace.

The African bishops thought an inordinate amount of time had been set aside for the British concerns and little or none for the others. They were in fact correct. The only items given time on the plenary schedule were the ordination of women and ecumenical relations until the African bishops requested a special plenary session to discuss the other concerns mentioned.

It is difficult to know who was feared most by the English bishops—the 175 African bishops or the other formidable block of bishops from ECUSA. In the end they have recognized that all of us are as concerned as they about the unity of the Anglican Communion. Interestingly enough it is primarily the English joined by some Africans and some other third world bishops who believe that the Anglican Communion faces an inevitable and irreparable split.

The emphasis at Lambeth has been generally one of deep concern for the future of this Communion, coupled with a profound yearning for a deepening of our spiritual lives. The day to day worship has reflected these concerns. The tone set by Archbishop Runcie has been one of unity and his every word has moved us closer together. I sense that what stands in the way of Anglican unity is a deep longing of many English bishops to see a reunion with the Vatican. Clearly at this stage they fail to see that true unity with Rome can only be found in a recognition of Anglican Orders. At present, the Pope is not prepared to do this. If the English Church agreed to unity on any other terms that would destroy the Anglican Communion as we now know it.

Further, there is a deep sense that many of the English bishops do not understand that in Anglicanism we all possess a "pearl of great price. " Because they do not understand, they underestimate its value. Whether the world likes it or not, England has had the greatest influence on human affairs of any country in the history of the world. That influence will continue for centuries, largely through that institution known as Anglicanism. If the Bishop of London and his friends should win the day, Anglicanism would come to an end, and the entire world would be poorer for that.

As we watch the waves of Anglicanism wash over Africa, make unheard of inroads in Central and South

America, and continue its reach into the Far East, I believe it to be the wave of the future. It is open, inclusive, and spiritually rich because of its diversity. It is rich in tradition and orthodoxy yet equally rich in its openness to new ideas, to new thoughts holding these in tension—orthodoxy and heterodoxy, thus fulfilling Elizabeth I's wise gift: "Say the Creed (orthodoxy), interpret it as you wish (heterodoxy), but let us not put windows in the souls of (people)."

While this is not an exact quotation, it does capture the spirit of the settlement of Elizabeth I that makes Anglicanism different. This is what the Anglican Communion offers to the world: a way to hold to the best of the Church's tradition; a way to strengthen the hold of scripture on our lives; and a way to release the Spirit from the stranglehold of tradition. It is, I believe, what the world needs.

Affectionately,
+John

Chapter 9

A Story to Tell to the Nations

Thou shalt judge the people righteously, and govern the nations upon the earth.—Psalm 67:4

When the definitive American history of the 20th century's second half is written, its principal theme will be the tumultuous story of an increasingly powerful country struggling to find its place among all the nations of the earth. There will be chapters on Central America, the Soviet Union, the Middle East. Generations of students to come will have to know what happened in Vietnam, Panama, Nicaragua, in Iran, Egypt, and Israel. They will need to understand men like Carter, Bush, and Reagan; like Tutu and Sadat. It is a shame they will not be able to debrief John Walker, for he was in the middle of it all. He went to places where history was being made; he knew the players firsthand. He watched as the foundations of the 21st century were laid.

For someone whose favorite job had been teaching American history, it must have been a thrill. Walker was an eyewitness to the United States' growing hegemony. He grew to manhood as the Second World War raged, went to school watching the Cold War bloom, found his voice protesting against the war in Vietnam, helped arrange the return of the Panama Canal to Panama, and of the Sinai peninsula to Egypt, received correspondence from hostages held by Islamic militants in Iran, rose to his full stature in opposing the nuclear arms race, and worked with the Senate on what to do about Nicaragua, Guatemala, and El Salvador. He died just a month and a few days before the Berlin Wall fell, and America was left as the world's only superpower.

But Bishop Walker did more than simply live close to the heart of affairs in interesting times. He seems almost to have been destined to stand as an interpreter and constructive critic of an era, as a kind of religious conscience for a country come of age. He was not content to let history unfold around the Church; he believed the Church was called to be an agent in making history.

His consciousness of that mission began on Easter Day 1937 as an eight-year-old boy waiting to be baptized. The last of several to join the Church that day, his immersion called forth "Amen!" and a doxology sang by 3,000 voices. It was a dynamic experience that marked him forever as Christ's own, reinforced when all those people marched by to shake his hand. As they marched, they were singing, too:

> We've a story to tell to the nations
> That will turn their hearts to the right.
> A story of love and mercy,
> A story of peace and light,
> A story of peace and light!
> And the darkness shall turn to dawning,
> And the dawning to noonday bright;
> And God's great kingdom shall come on earth,
> The kingdom of love and light.

Forty-six years later, he was still trying to understand the implications of that day. "I was not exactly sure what it meant, but clearly a good thing had happened to me," he wrote, describing that day on a riverbank in Michigan to a conference on Baptism and Ministry many years later.

The ministry of John Walker was devoted to bringing that "story of love and mercy" to the nations. Such a ministry may have been virtually inevitable for a history teacher rising to a place of ecclesiastical authority in the nation's capital. At the seat of power it was easy to be swept up into great events.

In 1969, John Walker was there when a quarter of a million college students marched for peace down Pennsylvania Avenue. They bore seven coffins filled with placards bearing the names of 40,000 U.S. soldiers who had died in Vietnam at that point. At the Cathedral two weeks later, Canon Walker remembered their coming:

> Recently, we were visited here by the largest crowd in history. Young Americans longing for peace, yearning for a togetherness that will cement human being to brother human being in a bond of mutual love and concern. In many ways it was a beautiful thing that was wrought here, and there surged in the hearts of all of us, and was spoken by writers who were present, a hope that maybe once again a little child, our collective children of peace, would lead us out of the darkness of hate and war into the bright ray of peace and a new adventure. But what they did not remember—and what perhaps we did not remember—was that when they sang "Where have all the flowers gone?" we already knew the answer to that disheartening question: in the hands of man, all purposes go awry, and all flowers go to graveyards.

His point was not to be pessimistic, or even to be realistic, though he was at times both.

"There is a savage beast in man that has to be tamed," he said. "Is it not enough," he asked, "to drive one to despair to catalogue the billions of ways in which man past or present has proved his inability to do whatever he does by himself?...[E]very hope goes awry, every dream is corrupted, every truth is crushed to earth, wrong rules and keeps men in separation." That is why, he argued, that individuals and nations needed a Wonderful Counselor, a Mighty God, an everlasting Father, a Prince of Peace to save us from our savage beastliness, to make way for the inner image of our own divinity to emerge.

In 1978, John Walker was there when Jimmy Carter faced the just but challenging task of convincing the U.S. Senate to approve the treaty returning control of the Panama Canal to the country that had been created to make its building possible. Walker sat on a presidential advisory board that helped develop public support for the Carter-Torrijos Treaty. (The treaty was ratified, and the canal reverted to Panamanian control on January 1, 2000.)

In 1979, John Walker was there on November 15 at 3 p.m. at the Cathedral when President Carter, Vice President Mondale, and Secretary of State Cyrus Vance joined the families of men and women who were being held by angry anti-American students in Tehran. He was there when the great organ began to play the "Battle Hymn of the Republic" as had been requested by the ranking diplomatic hostage in Iran, Charge d'Affaires Bruce Laingen. Thousands of worshipers joined in a spontaneous chorus. A prayer vigil began that afternoon that lasted *all* 444 days of his captivity. From his make-shift prison at the Iranian foreign ministry, Laingen later wrote the Bishop expressing his gratitude for the service. Walker prayed for the captives, for their families, and for the people of Iran and America, "that looking to the welfare of each other, we [might] come through anger and strife to reconciliation and friendship."

Five days later, John Walker was there when Anwar al-Sadat accepted the return of the Sinai peninsula from

Israel. He stood in the shadow of Mt. Sinai, the place where Jewish, Christian, and Muslim tradition holds that Moses received the Law. He surely agreed with Sadat, who saw in the Valley of Tuwa (the cradle of all three great monotheistic religions) "a great manifestation of the higher values upheld by mankind, namely those of tolerance and coexistence among all human beings." Two years later, after Sadat's assassination, John Walker was at the White House to deliver the invocation at a luncheon honoring the memory of the slain peacemaker.

John Walker was there at the "Bread Not Bombs" protest in a vacant lot among dilapidated houses on 14th Street in 1981. The Air Force Association had organized a display of sophisticated weaponry at a Washington, D.C. hotel. The Reagan revolution was underway, and as military spending soared Bishop Walker addressed a small crowd with revolutionary words of his own: "We have a choice: we must either halt the arms race or face annihilation." He launched a diocesan Commission on Peace, and in 1982 he turned himself, his staff, and the institutions he oversaw to the pursuit of nuclear disarmament. By 1985, cabinet secretaries, arms negotiators, ambassadors, generals, admirals, scientists, ethicists, and theologians had had their say. Bishop Walker testified before the U.S. Senate as a witness against nuclear proliferation and mutually assured destruction.

In 1983, John Walker was there when a grieving, shocked, and angry nation gathered at Washington Cathedral to mourn the victims of Korean Airlines Flight 007, "willfully shot out of the sky by a Soviet Air Force pilot," as he said, "a brutal act [that] plunged the civilized world into a pit of gloom and despair." A close friend of the Bishop's had been on board when the plane crashed into the Sea of Okhotsk just before dawn on

August 31. (A navigational error had put the flight path into Russian airspace.) He had visited with her three weeks before, when he had returned to Detroit for the 150th anniversary of the Diocese of Michigan. When he called in his sermon for the grief-stricken to forgive their enemies, his words were not some expected religious platitude, but rather evidence of a personal struggle of faith willingly shared with Presidents and Generals.

In 1987, John Walker was there when peace was trying to dawn in Central America. Having married a Costa Rican woman, he had a vested interest there. He worked the levers of government with an informal network of admirers (Episcopalian and otherwise). He supported the Arias agreements and the Guatemala Accords. He argued against military aide to the contras, while urging the United States to assume moral responsibility for them and their future settlement. He wrote articles on foreign policy that placed concern for human rights above economic and political philosophy. He urged cooperation, reflection, mutual understanding, dialogue, and good will. He eschewed both uninformed naiveté and the unilateral, doctrinal response of true believers, party functionaries, and ultra-nationalists.

In short, John Walker was there offering sanity and humanity whenever the nations of the earth contended. Uniquely placed in time and geography, he exercised an international ministry that joined pastoral and political affairs. He saw the atomic age dawn and waited in terror with the rest of the world to see if it would be the last sight ever seen. He was a first-row observer of the great battle between democracy and communism, and even though it was always clear what side he was on, he was not afraid to criticize both.

None of this is to say that John Walker considered

himself an expert in international affairs. He knew and said that he was no statesman, no military officer, no elected political leader. He respected the contributions of diplomats, soldiers, and politicians in the affairs of nations and in the keeping of the peace. But he insisted that the Church was called to have a voice in those affairs and that people of faith have a responsibility to work for peace among the nations.

These convictions arose from Walker's conviction that the Christ event, properly interpreted, is a clarion call for reconciliation—and not just the reconciliation of individuals with God, but also the reconciliation of the peoples of the world with each other. Walker understood that it is always the self that stands between us and God, and he understood as well that the nation is simply an extension of the self. He taught plainly that it is the elevation of self and nation—and the denigration of others and other nations that such elevation implies—that leads to separation and prevents peace. The self's desire for exaltation leads to separation, and separation is the first step on the road to war.

Christ came, John Walker taught, precisely to overcome the self's desire for ultimate supremacy by living a life of service and forgiveness that constituted a peace offering for the world. Christ came to lead the world from self-centeredness to self-sacrifice. As a result, the life of Christ breaks down the walls of enmity we build between ourselves and others. By his birth and death, Christ ends the "irrationality of separation" that divides friends, families, and nations. He comes "to create a new world, a new life, a new being out of the two that glared at each other across the no man's land where an uneasy truce keeps an uneasy peace." He took this "separated life of the world" unto himself, and "by absorbing it into his divinity" showed humankind "how to become a new creation, one being out of two with peace and liberty reigning within and without."

The theology is precise. But what made John Walker such a rare commodity was his ability to think clearly about complicated matters theologically while simultaneously translating his thought into practical policy. In 1978 Walker scribbled some notes on the last page of the briefing book on the Panama Canal treaties he received from the White House. (Bishop Walker was always scribbling in one book or the other—his library was filled with underlining, marginal notes, bits of poetry, and disputations.) It constitutes a Christian take on U.S. foreign policy, which he wrote "must not be seen simply in terms of self-interest but be seen in terms of justice," and be "based on sacred documents."

Throughout his life, John Walker struggled to make sense of the resurrection faith he knew to lie at the heart of his own believing. He grew in conviction that Christ came into history to bring abundant life to all, leaving no person or nation to be better than another, no people or peoples less the children of God than their neighbor. To him it made perfect sense. What made no sense to him, finally, was this: how is it, that in the face of such abundant life, the world is such a mess? In his 1983 Easter sermon, Bishop Walker asked:

> Why then do we hate? Why do wars persist? Why do so few of us have so much and so many have so little? Why do we force small nations to rise up in revolution to gain redress of their grievances, many of which we laid on them ourselves? If we intervene in the name of justice, or merely for our own best interests, why do we come with weapons bringing more death?

He concluded, sadly, that the failure of nations to be reconciled to each other was a failure by the Church to take the meaning of the resurrection seriously and to communicate its central truth clearly to the world. The blame lay with Christians' failure, he believed, to think of resurrection as being a present reality, as happening every day.

"Whenever we reach out in understanding to others, whether friend or foe, resurrection happens," he said, his voice rising in confidence and falling into an unexpected cadence. "Christ is risen. Whenever we see the city of God being built in justice and peace, resurrection is in progress. Christ is risen," he went on. Resurrection, he explained, was also surely yet to come. Yet he believed that "if it isn't happening now, then we needn't worry about it"—resurrection, he believed was meant to be a promise, but much more so, a reality.

He could conclude his Easter sermon, and his life, with a Christian call to arms that proclaims the only news that nations need to hear, the only story ultimately worth telling:

> Let us walk in the light of the resurrection so that God's love may grasp us and we may be transformed and in turn may transform the world, so that weapons may indeed be beaten into plowshares and men and women not study war anymore. In Christ we say all things are possible. Do we believe that? Then let us begin to act as though it were true. Let us rejoice. Let us embrace one another as children of reconciliation and go forth together. And together we will know peace, and together we can build here in our time the marvelous city of God.

National Cathedral's Christmas Day broadcast is among the longest running religious programs on television. That service is the context for this 1979 sermon, delivered not quite two months after sixty-six Americans had been taken hostage in Iran by militant supporters of the Islamic fundamentalist Ayatollah Ruhollah Khomeini. No one knew the hostage crisis would last an incredible 444 days, becoming a focus of national anger and grief that clouded the final year of the Carter administration and framed the 1980 presidential election.

Good morning to you all. I think it is wonderful of you to come to be with us here at the National Cathedral so early on Christmas morning. Most children are at home opening their presents or perhaps watching this service on their TV sets. Merry Christmas to you and to them.

The Cathedral is especially beautiful today with color, of red and green and with the sound of the choir and organ raised in beautiful Christmas songs. What I want to do now is to tell you and the children who are watching and listening at home what Christmas is about. I know, you will say that you know what Christmas is about. Why, you've been watching TV shows about Christmas everyday for several weeks now. Some of you will probably say that it is about Santa Claus, reindeer, decorated trees, toys that talk, shining stars, snowflakes, and such things. Others will say that it is about gifts and happiness and angels singing. And all of you would be partly right. Of course, we know that toys don't really talk, except maybe computers. We know that reindeer can't fly and that Christmas is only about snowflakes in places where it is cold enough to have snow.

But you also know that Christmas is about God. It is about light. It is about a baby. A real live baby who was born a long time ago in a far away place. His name is Jesus and we believe him to be the Son of God, given by God to everybody as his gift, as his light for the world and to be his love for his people.

Christmas is about Mary and Joseph going to Bethlehem where she would have her baby. It is about Jesus being born in a manger, in a cow's stall because there was no room for them in the inn. Do you know what an inn is? It is a place where people taking a trip may stop for the night, to eat and sleep. Do you remember how the story goes?

> And there were in the same country shepherds in the field keeping watch over their sheep by night. And suddenly, the angel of the Lord came upon them, and the glory of the Lord shone round about them: and they were so afraid.
>
> And the angel said unto them, do not be afraid: For, behold, I bring you good tidings of great joy, which shall be to all people.
>
> For unto you is born this day in the city of David a Savior, which is Christ the Lord.
>
> And this shall be a sign unto you; ye shall find the babe wrapped in swaddling clothes, lying in a manger.
>
> And suddenly there was with the angel a great number of the heavenly hosts praising God, and saying,
>
> Glory to God in the Highest, and on earth peace, good will toward Men.

We began with the prophetic pronouncement of Isaiah that, "The people who walked in the darkness have seen a great light, they that dwell in the land of the shadow of death, upon them hath the light shined." St. Luke called us to "Look up and lift up our heads for our redemption draweth night." St. John picks up the light theme. In the Gospel he writes: "In the beginning was the word and the word was God. In Him was life and the life was the light of men." And further along he says, "The light shineth in the darkness and the darkness did not overcome it."

Our theme is light: God's light; the light of a star; the light of Christ. It is the light that dispels the dark of doubt and confusion. It is the light that overcomes fear of the unknown. It is the light which reveals truth and meaning. It is the light that brings understanding. It is by the light of Christ that God's love is demonstrated to a world often caught in the darkness of hate and war.

We are led to Bethlehem by the light of a star and there we find Him who is the light of the world. But it is not only in Bethlehem that we find him. He is to be found wherever women and men of faith gather. He is to be found in the cities of unbelief, where dwell those who are unable to believe because of our poor witness. He is to be found among the hungry, the imprisoned, the exile. Yes, my friends, he is to be found in Tehran in the embassy there and in the foreign office. He is the light in the temporary darkness that surrounds those held therein. He is the light and hope of those who pray daily for their safe return home. He is *our* light in this nation. He *will* light everyone who comes into the world. There is much more to be said about light but I would like to close this homily by reading a message from Mr. Bruce Laingen, the Charge d'Affaires in Tehran. His family and the families of many of the hostages are worshiping here with us on Christmas Day. Bruce Laingen writes:

> Together with our colleagues held in silent hostage in Tehran, we are one with you this morning in welcoming again the great promise of the Christmas message.
> We join with you, in the words of St. John's gospel, in welcoming the promise of that Light that

shines in the darkness. And we join with you, in the voices of the Angels, in celebration of this day of new birth and new hope in the promise of peace on earth and good will among men.

May that Light of Christmas and that promise of peace strengthen each of us to face every challenge with courage and every disappointment with hope. And in the words of St. Paul, may God from the wealth of His glory give us power through His spirit to be strong in our inner selves.

We extend to you our grateful thanks for your support, your good will, and your prayers—above all for your Cathedral's vigil prayer for the ultimate triumph of reconciliation and brotherhood that is the promise of both the Muslim and Christian faith.

And so *we* end as we began—

The people who walked in darkness
Have seen a great light.
Those that dwell in the land of
The Shadow of death
Upon them hath the Light shined
Look up—Lift up your heads your
          redemption draweth nigh.

This meditation written in December 1981, provides a rare glimpse into the private thoughts of John Walker: bishop, historian, father, theologian, activist, mystic. His reflections on a quiet drive through Virginia's countryside provide insight into Walker's humanity.

On the eve of All Saints' Day 1981, I was driving along Route 3 in Virginia on my way from St. Paul's, Piney, to Charlottesville to attend the last hours of Parents' Day at the University of Virginia. I had just attended a very exciting meeting of the Region Six Assembly. We had discussed with a sense of interdependence the serious economic problems that all of us in parishes and the Diocese must face together.

We had looked at the budget forecast for 1982 and at our potential response to the growing needs of people in our various communities. We had, further, explored the opportunity to expand our ministry to the aging by assisting in the development of a life care community.

All of this was on my mind as the signs began to appear giving directions to Chancellorsville, the Wilderness, Fredericksburg, and other memorials to that awful American war known as the Civil War, the War Between the States, and euphemistically known as the irrepressible conflict.

It was not the fact of its being All Hallows Eve that turned my mind from Piney to thoughts of the dead. Rather, it was the deep sense of history and presence that momentarily captured my thoughts.

Looking at the ground all around and at the arrows pointing toward the battlefields, I could not help identifying with the dead of that war. The still, green earth is enriched by the blood of so many of the young men of a nation. The thought then came that it didn't matter on which side they had fought. Each side had fought what it believed to be an honorable war for justice and truth and liberty. Both sides believed that they were doing God's will. In what is for us an incomprehensible way, both believed that they were fighting and dying as Christians for human freedom.

As I drove along, I thought that I could hear their voices and see their bodies dying and dead. Then two questions came—Was it forever thus? Is it forever to be?

From the beginning of time until now men have fought, threatened and killed each other to protect and defend; to gain more wealth; to expand land and power. They have fought and killed for revenge and to guarantee freedom. It was ever thus! The Old Testament is replete with such skirmishes and wars. From Babylonia, Persia and Egypt to Peloponesus, to Rome and England, all that time from Moses to Jesus, time itself was identified and marked off by strife and war.

We Christians would like to believe that the coming of Jesus, whom we worship as the Christ, the Prince of Peace, made a difference. We would like to believe that wars became less frequent; that somehow *men* changed, and all that makes for war vanished and peace became a possibility.

Historically, we know better. The birth of Christianity made an enormous difference in the world, but war did not cease. From A.D. 70 to Afghanistan 1980, the madness has continued. We could list more than a few major ones: Rome, England and Spain, the Crusades, the Reformation Wars, Jeanne d'Arc's wars, the English-Spanish battle for the mastery of the seas, the French Indian Wars, the American Revolution, England and India, German unification, Italian unification, the Russo-Japanese War, WWI, WWII, Korea, Vietnam, Israel and Egypt. On and on they march.

Chancellorsville and Fredericksburg were simply the moment of *recalling* and the moment of active reliving of an event that involved all of us personally. Each time I drive past such a battleground, I relive that important time in American History. On each occasion, I have a dramatic experience of anamnesis (recall and remembrance) and of the meaning of the communion of saints. Later that night, I found myself reciting the names of family, friends, students, and others who had died in recent wars (mostly in their youth).

In the two-hour drive back to Washington, I was made aware once again that Christ came to forgive sinners: to reconcile us to God and to break down the walls that we have erected. He was born to bring peace into our chaos and to forgive us every sin. He came to call us back to ourselves as found in Him and to thus restore the image to its fullness.

As we now approach Advent, I pray that we will reexamine what it means to be Christian in a world filled with warring madness and fraught with such fearsome dangers. I pray also that we will meditate on what it means to worship the Prince of Peace in a world that has in times past named a slave prison "Fort Jesus" and more recently named a submarine the "Corpus Christi!"

All Saints' Day 1981 is behind us, but let us take note that too many men and women have died in vain; that too many children of the earth have been victims of greed and aggrandizement. Let us remember each day that our *failure* to heed His call to oneness has brought us to the dark abyss of war. That massive array of the saints, living and dead, is watching and waiting for us to bring to an end the madness of those who lead us and protect us unto death.

On October 9, 1981, Bishop Walker offered this prayer at a White House luncheon honoring the memory of slain Egyptian President Anwar al-Sadat. In 1979 Walker had traveled with an American delegation sent by President Jimmy Carter, to witness the return of the Sinai to Egypt. The return was a gesture that followed Sadat's historic visit to Israel and the subsequent agreements reached at Camp David in 1978. Sadat was assassinated as he watched an annual military parade.

O God, you have made us in your image, and in every age you have sent men and women to lead your people along the pathway of justice and truth. Look with compassion on us who occupy this fragile island home. Help us to know that we only do your will when we overcome those things that divide us. Help us to see that it is love alone that can keep us from falling into the trap of self-centered superiority.

We give you thanks for this land and for the freedom and security that we have known over the years. We thank you for a government in which our leaders do not lord it over the people, and we thank you for the strong and decent men and women who come among us from time to time and who serve as a reminder that it is on the shoulders of ordinary people that the institutions of government are built.

Protect our leaders and our people from the suddenness of death by terrorism, and grace our friends, the people of Egypt, with your presence in their deep agony. Reach out in compassion to them and grant your merciful forgiveness to those who commit crimes against others. May they and we be led into truth, that the causes of our separation being overcome, we may at last find unity and peace. Amen.

Israel invaded Lebanon in the summer of 1982 in an attempt to secure its northern border from Palestinian guerillas. Later that fall, Lebanese Christian Phalangist president Bashir Gemayel was assassinated by Syrian agents. Within a week, local militia loyal to Gemayel entered the Sabra and Shatila refugee camps outside Beirut, where a multinational mix of people had fled following the Israeli siege of the capital. Apparently within sight of Israeli military authorities, the militia took their revenge with a three-day-long massacre. Many hundreds died. The slaughter occasioned international outrage. In an interfaith service of protest and remembrance held on the National Mall, Bishop Walker gave this statement.

The massacre of the Palestinian people, men, women, babies, and old people in Beirut would have been beyond belief, had we not seen the results of it in our own homes through television. It was a shattering experience. In the strongest terms possible we must condemn the acts of those who committed and abetted the butchery. We forget the lessons of history at our own peril; for this holocaust in Beirut is only the most recent example of the extent of callous brutality, cruelty, and hardness of heart which human beings are capable of expressing. Moreover, we must sadly acknowledge that such a tragedy is the inevitable consequence of the hidden and open evil within the human heart. Arrogance, group hatred and prejudice, aloofness to the suffering of others and the tolerance of oppression — are not these the roots which bear such evil fruit?

I bid you, members of the Episcopal Diocese of Washington, and all who will listen, to come into the presence of the God of Peace, confess the sin that is in us all and ask for forgiveness. Let us pray for the peoples in Lebanon, particularly the Palestinian survivors of the carnage. Let us also give of our resources to help in the rebuilding of their lives. In that regard I urge you to send gifts to the Presiding Bishop's Fund for World Relief earmarked for the Middle East.

My friends, confession and prayer, however sincere, gifts however generous, are worth little unless they are the beginning of a constant, determined concern for peace and justice in the Middle East, in Central America, and wherever there is war and oppression. And let us not forget our need for peace and justice in America.

Christ died in every child and every person killed in that massacre. However, in Christ's death there is always new life and redemption. Let us work so that from the great suffering in Beirut may yet come a resurrection. May the spirit of hope replace fear, forgiveness overcome vengeance, and new communities arise where justice, peace, and freedom prevail. Blessed be the peacemakers. Bless you my friends.

Chapter 10

A Great National Church

Render to Caesar the things that are Caesar's, and to God the things that are God's.—Mark 12:17

At precisely 10:58 a.m., four-thousand people stood up as the President of the United States was escorted to his seat. He was led by a solemn-looking man who wore a floor-length purple robe and carried the authoritative staff of Cathedral verger. The organ roared to life as cross and torches entered the great church, and the congregation sang out its thanks and prayers: "God of our fathers whose Almighty hand…In this free land by thee our lot is cast…Thy word our law, thy paths our chosen way… Be thy strong arm our ever sure defense."

Then John Walker led the assembled crowd in the ancient antiphonal psalm that almost certainly was used thousands of years ago to anoint the Chosen People's king:

> V: *I was glad when they said to me, "We will go into the house of the Lord."*
> R: *Our feet shall stand in your gates, O Jerusalem.*
>
> V: *O Lord, your word endures forever in heaven.*
> R: *Your truth remains from one generation to another.*
>
> V: *Nations shall come to your light.*
> R: *And kings to the brightness of your rising.*

The United States decided early on against a monarchy, and only a little later disavowed state-supported religion. But in 1989, George Herbert Walker Bush, the new President of United States, was about as close as you could get to an American monarch. When he went to pray at the Washington Cathedral, Church and State came close together.

Two-hundred years before, the American people had inaugurated their first Chief Executive, another good vestryman in what would become the Episcopal Church in the United States of America. That first George did not hesitate to invoke the Almighty, either. At his inauguration in 1789, Washington added the words "So help me God" to the thirty-five word Oath of Office mandated by the Constitution. In 1989, George H.W. Bush would—like every President between the first and the forty-first—make the same addition.

Two days after Bush stood opposite Chief Justice William H. Rehnquist on Capitol Hill, he sat across from Bishop John Thomas Walker in the crossing of the Cathedral Church of St. Peter and St. Paul. Four years earlier, Bush had been in attendance as Vice President when the Cathedral held its first National Prayer Service for the second inauguration of Ronald W. Reagan.

In 1985, Reagan's Inaugural Committee had contacted the Cathedral about the possibility of holding a service to pray for the nation's newly-elected leader. Fresh off an electoral victory of historic proportion, Reagan and his advisors were seeking ways to bring their fiery brand of social and political conservatism more into the mainstream of American life. What better way could there be to re-locate the then firmly-established power of the Moral Majority than to televise the movement's lead spokesman, the Rev. Jerry Falwell, in the distinguished Canterbury

Pulpit in that most established of Churches, the Cathedral of the Episcopal Diocese of Washington. It would have been a perfect symbol—except that Bishop Walker would have none of it. After high-level negotiations, the more moderate dean of American evangelical Christianity, the Rev. Billy Graham, was called to preach at Reagan's inaugural prayer service instead. Even the august Dr. Graham was not allowed to speak on that frigid January morning in 1985 until the text of his sermon had been pre-approved by the Dean of the Cathedral, Bishop Walker.

Not surprisingly, when his neighbor and fellow Episcopalian George H.W. Bush was elected president in 1988, Bishop Walker moved to take the initiative for holding an inaugural prayer service of his own design. Just one day after the November general election, Walker sent the invitation to hold such a service at the National Cathedral to Bush's official residence at the Naval Observatory, just a few blocks from the Walker's Northwest Washington home. Bush's acceptance was not long in coming, and by Christmas, a clear plan for the service was in place.

Prayer, music, scripture, and preaching would be gracefully arranged by Bishop Walker in a delicate balance between Christian faith and political responsibility. The liturgy struck three themes: caring for America, caring for God's creation, and reconciling the people of the earth. Although he spoke beyond the printed liturgy only to welcome the congregation and their distinguished guests, John Walker expressed his idea of the Church's relationship to the State with every note played and every speaker heard that day. Moving characteristically both out front and behind the scenes, Walker managed no mean feat. With one hand, he blessed the new administration. With the other, he pointed high above some of the most powerful men on Earth, reminding them that they, too, were accountable both to their constituents and to their Creator.

Walker did not preach to the President. He asked the Episcopal Church's Presiding Bishop to give the homily that day. Edmund Browning, just a few months earlier, had defeated him in a close election to become the highest ranking bishop in the Episcopal Church.

In some respects, the Bush Inaugural Prayer Service represents in John Walker the culmination of a lifetime of thinking and acting on the relationship between Church and State. In his youth, Walker became disenchanted with the Church. Leaving behind personal piety and organized religion, he was caught up in the first waves of young men who pressed urgently for the civil rights and economic opportunity of African-Americans. The first years of Walker's university career at Wayne State were devoted to protests against segregation and racial discrimination. As he drifted away from the African Methodist Episcopal Zion churches of his childhood, the young Walker drifted into the Episcopal Church. There he found a community of faith which could encompass both personal religious experience and liberal political activism.

One of Walker's earliest national commitments was to the National Coalition for Public Education and Religious Liberty (PEARL), an umbrella group of educational, religious, and civil liberties organizations dedicated to preserving the wall of separation between Church and State. He served as the organization's President in the early 1970s. Walker's credentials as an educator and church leader were becoming well established, and as a condition of office, he became a member of the American Civil Liberties Union.

As PEARL's representative, Walker made his first entry into the world of politics on a national scale. In the fall of 1974 the organization planned to meet in Washington, and they hoped to bring their concerns to the Oval Office. Unfortunately, Gerald Ford had arrived there himself less than a week before their letter crossed his desk, and under somewhat difficult circumstances. Their request was politely denied. PEARL tried again in late November, this time with a letter from Walker, hoping perhaps that the Bishop Suffragan of Washington might receive a more sympathetic hearing from the new Episcopal President. It did not.

Yet barely two years later, Bishop Walker would walk down the steps of the National Cathedral between Mrs. Betty Ford and HRH Prince Philip as they left together from the great celebration of English and American community held there to celebrate the nation's Bicentennial. His ministry brought him in close contact with every subsequent president. The intensely religious man who stood to defend the constitutional barrier between politics and religion was intensely, intentionally political.

And he was highly visible as well. Twice Walker prayed to open the legislative day of the U.S. Senate. He graced the dedication of the National Gallery's new East Wing with a meaningful and carefully crafted prayer of dedication. He preached in celebration of the Treaty of Paris (1783) that ended the Revolutionary War. He sat on a panel to review the process of judicial appointments in the District of Columbia. He marched on the East Central steps of the Capitol to oppose amendments to the Constitution regarding prayer in public schools. He joined the debate about a crèche on the Mall near the National Christmas Tree and its accompanying Pageant of Peace. Long before poll-driven presidencies, a young Cathedral

Canon warned about the dangers of government by opinion polling.

Taken together, Walker's growing sense of responsibility and his increasing confidence on the national stage left him quite highly involved in affairs of state—for a man who called for the Church carefully to be separated from all government influence.

Walker's understanding of that separation was deeply historical. As a teacher of United States history, he was well aware of the intricate role that religion played in the development of the American Republic. Over the years, he spoke eloquently and at some length about the Church and its role in a democratic society. His clearest statement came in a 1981 lecture at the Church of the Holy Trinity on Rittenhouse Square in Philadelphia. It was an unusual place for a black bishop from Georgia, a man who prayed with Presidents, to speak against tuition tax credits for the parents of parochial school children, to denounce challenges to the tax-exempt status of religious organizations that engaged in the political process, and to repeat his opposition to state-mandated prayer in the public schools.

Walker believed that the separation of church and state could be carried too far. He saw the framers of the Constitution as being concerned "that there be no covenant between the government and any religious body that might reproduce the European madness of an established religion." In Walker's view, the purpose of the First Amendment was to guarantee that every religion would "have equal opportunity to survive and grow without support or hindrance."

This moderate view left Walker open to be intimately involved with political leaders and constructively engaged in the political process while at the same time preserving his own—and the Church's—moral independence. In the decade of the Moral Majority's greatest influence on American politics, Walker faulted conservative Christians not for their desire to engage in national policymaking, but rather for the methods and content of their engagement. Walker would countenance no endorsement of specific candidates for office, nor would he use a candidate's professed religious beliefs or affiliations as litmus tests for the support of Christian voters. He refused to make one or two hot-button issues into political shibboleths designed to identify candidates worthy of the Church's support.

The essentially dynamic relationship between church and state is no less real for us than it was during the days of John Walker's ministry. In this most religious of modern societies, Walker's principled approach to church-state relations deserves continued study and application. He preached and practiced a strong commitment to the religious pluralism he understood as lying at the heart of the First Amendment. He insisted on a global perspective for decision-making. He called for clear thinking and knowledgeable discussion of substantive public policy issues within the context of the community of faith. He believed that Christians were called to be actively engaged in the political process, and he understood every morally justifiable advance in history to have been the result of such engagement. He refused an easy distinction between sacred and secular, arguing that "every act we perform...is in a deep sense sacred and must be addressed by God's people for God's people and for the world."

He anchored this political philosophy in a carefully grounded theology of the People of God and their covenant relationship with the One who is sovereign over every political process and institution. He praises Isaiah for forcing on his people "the hard truth about their heritage" and for warning them of the dire consequences of "being lulled unto illusion by mere abundance and prosperity." He calls on the nation to repent in the face of "the fragility of wealth and the inconsistency and fickleness of power." For Walker, the past was merely a mirror of the present and a springboard into the future. Whenever he taught about Church and State he was looking for the world to come.

In Walker's mind, the fulfillment of that dream required participation, education, and above all, repentance. He searched again and again for a way to explain how the ideals of the American Republic (and the Kingdom of God which they reflected) had fallen so short in the pragmatic world of politics and international relations. Was it a lack of will, a deficit of understanding, a fundamental confusion about what is good and just in the world? At one time or another, Walker suggested each of these weighty explanations for the world's sad state of affairs.

But in the end he offered that most classically Anglican of answers, echoing great 20th century English theologians like William Temple, Archbishop of Canterbury during the heart of the Second World War. Our failure as Christians, and as Americans, to live out our founders' dream lies squarely at the feet of our self-satisfying demand to place ourselves at the center of the universe, to place our own needs above the needs of others, to seek our own good rather than that which is best for all. In other ages, this primary fault was called original sin. Written in the language of nations, Walker knew, first-hand, it spelled the disastrous course of history throughout most of the twentieth century.

"The failure of humanity to achieve peace," Walker wrote, "is tied to our failure to recognize our need for confession and forgiveness. We commit ghastly crimes against each other, both as individuals and as nations, and in the end, we struggle never to look back, never to remember. As we surge forward, we suddenly discover that we are hampered by past sins; by the other's ability to forget the past; by our own inability to confess. And so reconciliation does not take place, and peace slips from us again."

Looking forward in the twenty-first century, this cycle of unforgiven sin, described by a man whose episcopacy was dedicated to reconciliation, seems depressingly familiar. The world is no less dangerous than it was in 1968 when Canon Walker was trying to explain to a congregation of largely white Episcopalians why so many young black men were angry in America. The answer, he explained, lay in a gap between what Christian America said and did, a division that had produced a generation filled with anger. He was still young himself, still questioning the establishment into which he was entering ever more deeply. It was a habit he would continue to the end.

His words contain echoes of the radical theology of the mid 1960s, and he quotes John F. Kennedy with an obvious reverence that the revelations of recent years would probably have made less gilded. But his message is still essentially filled with hope and an urgent call to action:

> If we claim to be a land of the free, then we must be that. If we are peacock proud of our gross national product, and we are, then no one should be hungry. No one should be jobless who wants to work. No child should have a toothache because he can't afford a dentist. If we are truly Christian and believe in peace, then we must

move mountains to achieve that goal. If we truly love people everywhere, then war must cease and injustice must die.

The answer of the ancient Church for itself and the world was death. Now we would bypass all the unpleasantness of the crucifixion and go straight to the resurrection. But in this there is no power. Death is the Church's answer to itself and to the world: the death of hate, the death of dishonesty, the death of war, the death of injustice, the death of the ego-centered self. Only by this can we become who we are, what we claim to be: the land of the free, the brave new world, the fulfillment of humankind's utopian dream.

Can we do this? I don't know. But in the words of the late President John F. Kennedy, "let us at least begin."

> O wounded hands of Jesus, build
> In us thy new creation;
> Our pride is dust, our vaunt is stilled,
> We wait thy revelation:
> O love that triumphs over loss,
> We bring our hearts before thy cross,
> To finish thy salvation.

Fifteen years later, Walker would stand outside the Cathedral to dedicate the Reconciliation Cross which sits at the apex of the West Front. He dedicated it "in the firm belief that the God of Abraham, Isaac, and Jacob calls us to [be reconciled]. We do so in the belief that the Prophets, the prayer of Muhammad, and the life of Christ all point toward peace and reconciliation."

"We hear it said again and again that we have to begin somewhere. We invite you to join us here and now in our search for reconciliation and peace. Let us not shrink from the discussion of even the most difficult subjects—

let us talk of an end to racial antagonism; let us talk of disarmament openly and without fear; let us pray with all oppressed people. Let us raise up this cross to tower above this city. Let it remind us always that our true ministry is not finally against anyone, but rather it is for justice, truth, and peace in reconciling love for everyone."

The Reconciliation Cross stands today as a fitting symbol of Walker's ideal of the way to understand the relationship between Church and State.

The Bishop John T. Walker Biography Committee

Acknowledgements

Many of John Walker's friends and admirers have assisted in the research, funding, production, and marketing of this biography and for that support we are deeply grateful. They include:

Hugh Adams
George Allen
Craig Anderson
George Baker
David Beers
Jon Bruno
Julian Bull
Lloyd Casson
John Chane
Peter Cheney
Charles Clark
Doyt Coon
Paul Cooney
Kortright Davis
Charles Demere
The Diocese of Washington
Dalton Downs
Ted Eastman
Jim Fenhagen
Bitsy Folger
Ray Foote
The Forrester Clark Foundation
Forward Movement
John Frizzell
Dennis Fruitt
Carlson Gerdau
Jonathan Glass
Ted Gleason
Frank Griswold
Ed Hall
Preston Hannibal
Barbara Harris
Robert Harrison
Pat Hass
Betsy Holleman
Martha Horne
Amo Houghton

Norman Hull
Derrick Humphries
Jonca Humphries
Joan Jewett
Kathryn Lasseron
The Lee and Juliet Folger Fund
Richard Lee
Margaret Lewis
Heath Light
Clark Lobenstine
James Lowe
Bill Matthews
Bob McLean
Lily McLean
Tina Meade
Jim Naughton
Benjamin Neilson
Ryan Newman
Charles Perry
Nathaniel Porter
Dora Richardson
Greg Rixon
Evie Rooney
St. Paul's School
Margot Semler
Kwasi Thornell
Phyllis Tickle
George Tracey
Brad Turner
Desmond Tutu
The Union of Black Episcopalians
Virginia Theological Seminary
The Walker Family
Washington National Cathedral
Cheryl Daves Wilburn
Juan Williams
Wesley Williams